NEW

Total English

STARTER

Workbook with Key

Jonathan Bygrave

Contents

Vocabulary | international words

1 Match the words from the box with the photos.

> bus   chocolate   computer   doctor
> ~~passport~~   pizza   restaurant   taxi
> telephone   television

_____passport_____

_____

_____

_____

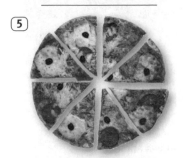

_____

_____

_____

_____

_____

_____

Speaking

2 **a** Complete the dialogues with the words in the box.

> Welcome   too   My   I'm   ~~Nice~~   name   Hi

1 **A:** Hello. I'm Dave Reed.
   B: Hello. I'm Usha Kapoor. _Nice_ to meet you.
   A: Nice to meet you, (1) _____ .
2 **A:** Hi, Mona.
   B: (2) _____ , Andre.
3 **A:** Hello. (3) _____ to Hotel Presidente.
   B: Thank you. (4) _____ name is Claire Aston.
4 **A:** Hello. I'm Charles. What's your (5) _____ ?
   B: (6) _____ Taku.
   A: Welcome to London Tours, Taku.

b Match the pictures (A–D) with the dialogues in exercise 2a.

A

Dialogue _2_

B

Dialogue ___

C

Dialogue ___

D

Dialogue ___

Listening

3 🔘 02 Listen and complete the dialogues.

1 **A:** Hello.
  B: Hi.
  A: I'm Edward. What's your name?
  B: (1) _____ _____ Jane.
  A: Nice to meet you.
  B: (2) _____ _____ _____ _____ ,
     _____ .

2 **A:** Hello. Welcome to Hotel Idris.
  B: (3) _____ _____ .
  A: What's your name?
  B: (4) _____ _____ Rosa Lane.

3 **A:** (5) _____ .
  B: Hello.
  A: (6) _____ _____ _____ ?
  B: I'm Sergio.
  A: (7) _____ _____ _____ _____ ,
     Sergio. (8) _____ Selina.
  B: Nice to meet you, too, Selina.

Pronunciation | /aɪ/

4 🔘 03 Listen and underline the /aɪ/ sounds in the dialogue.

A: <u>Hi</u>. <u>My</u> name's Don. What's your name?
B: Hello, Don. I'm Judy.
A: Nice to meet you, Judy.
B: Nice to meet you too, Don.

Grammar | to be: I and you

5 Complete the dialogues with *I'm* or *you're*.

A: Hello. My name's Pierre. What's your name?
B: *I'm* Julie.

1 **A:** Hello. (1) _____ Adam Gorski.
  B: Welcome to Hotel Lux, Mr Gorski.
  A: Thank you.
  B: (2) _____ in room 8-1-8.

2 **A:** Hello, (3) _____ Clive Wells.
  B: Nice to meet you, Clive. (4) _____ Lori.
  A: Nice to meet you, too, Lori.

6 Find four more mistakes in the dialogues and correct them.

A: Hello. ɫ Svetlana Rochev. *I'm*
B: Hello, Ms Rochev. ✓

1 **A:** Good morning, Mr Nakamura. You in room 9-2-2. ____
  B: Thank you. ____

2 **A:** Hello. Im Jin Chang. ____
  B: Im Farah Coleman. ____

3 **A:** I'm John Wilson. ____
  B: Hello, Mr Wilson. Youre in room 1-0-2. ____

Vocabulary | numbers 0–10

7 **a** Write the numbers in the correct order.

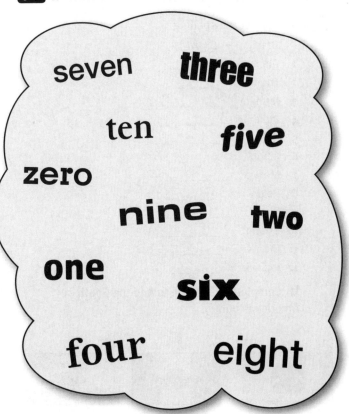

zero, one, _____

b Complete the crossword.

Across →	Down ↓
b 10	a 2
d 1	c 8
f 5	e 4
h 6	g 7
i 3	
j 9	

a
b | T |
  | W | c
d | O | e
   f
   g
   h
i
j

Vocabulary | countries

1 **a** Correct the spelling.

Brasil *Brazil*

1 Chine _____
2 Franse _____
3 Jermany _____
4 Indie _____
5 Italie _____
6 Japon _____
7 Mexica _____
8 Polan _____
9 Rusia _____
10 Espain _____
11 the YK _____
12 the OSA _____

b Complete the puzzle to find the South American country.

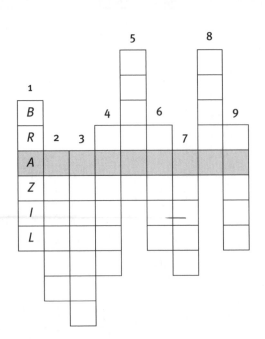

How to... | ask where someone is from

2 **a** Put the words in the correct order to make a dialogue.

A: from, you Ben? Where are
   Where are _____ _____ _____

B: Poland. from I'm
   _____ _____ _____

A: in Where Poland?
   _____ _____ _____

B: Warsaw.
   _____

b Write dialogues. Use the prompts.

1 Kana / Japan / Tokyo
   A: *Where are you from, Kana?*
   B: _____
   A: _____
   B: _____

2 Javier / Mexico / Mexico City
   A: _____
   B: _____
   A: _____
   B: _____

3 Ilya / Russia / Moscow
   A: _____
   B: _____
   A: _____
   B: _____

Grammar | to be: he, she and it

3 Write dialogues for each picture.

Sergio — Spain

A: *Who's he?*
B: *He's Sergio.*
A: *Where's he from?*
B: *He's from Spain.*

Amy — UK

1
A: _____
B: _____
A: _____
B: _____

Francesca — Italy

2
A: _____
B: _____
A: _____
B: _____

Calvin — USA

3
A: _____
B: _____
A: _____
B: _____

4 Write two sentences for each picture. Use the prompts.

 (He/Mexico) *He isn't from Mexico. He's from Brazil.*

 1 (She/Spain) _____

_____ .

 2 (He/Italy) _____

_____ .

3 (She/Russia) _____

_____ .

4 (He/Turkey) _____

_____ .

5 Write dialogues. Use the prompts.

car/BMW/Mercedes

A: *Nice car!*

B: *Thanks!*

A: *Is it a BMW?*

B: *No, it isn't. It's a Mercedes.*

1 computer/a Dell/an Apple

A: _____

B: _____

A: _____

B: _____

2 telephone/a Nokia/a Motorola

A: _____

B: _____

A: _____

B: _____

3 television/a Sony/a Panasonic

A: _____

B: _____

A: _____

B: _____

Pronunciation | contractions

6 a Rewrite the sentences using contractions.

I am from the UK and he is from the USA.

I'm from the UK and he's from the USA.

1 Who is he and where is he from?

_____

2 It is not from Italy. It is from Spain.

_____

3 I am from Poland and you are from Germany.

_____

b 🔊 04 Listen and check. Then say the sentences.

Reading

7 Read the dialogue and complete the details about the three people.

Receptionist: Hello. Welcome to Fortune Hotel.

Jane: Thank you.

Receptionist: What's your name, please?

Jane: I'm Jane Jones. Now, where's my passport? Oh, here it is.

Receptionist: Thank you. You're in room six-one-four, Ms Jones. And what's your name?

Paul: I'm Paul Earle.

Receptionist: Is this your passport, Mr Earle?

Paul: Yes, it is.

Receptionist: OK. You're in room eight-one-nine, Mr Earle.

Paul: OK, thank you.

Jane: Hey, Paul, who's she?

Paul: Who? Oh, she's Candy Fox.

Jane: Candy Fox? Is she a celebrity?

Paul: Yes, she is. She's from the USA.

Jane: New York?

Paul: No. She's from Los Angeles.

1

Name: _____

Room: _____

2

Name: _____

Room: _____

3

Name: _____

From: _____

Vocabulary | nationalities

1 Complete the table with the nationality of the countries in the box.

> ~~Brazil~~   China   Germany   India   Italy
> Japan   Mexico   Poland   Russia   Spain
> the UK   the USA

-ian/an	-ish	-ese
Brazilian	_____	_____
_____	_____	_____
_____		
_____		
_____		
_____		

2 Label the flags.

the Japanese flag

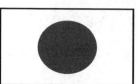
1   _____

2   _____

3   _____

4   _____

5   _____

3 Look at the profile. Complete the sentences about Carmina.

File   Edit   View   Go   Bookmarks   Tools   Help

Carmina Moretti

1   **From:** Italy
2   **Favourite food:** Kung Pao chicken (from China)
3   **Favourite film:** _Four Weddings and a Funeral_ (from the UK)
4   **Favourite singer:** Lady Gaga (from the USA)
5   **Favourite actor:** Gael Garcia Bernal (from Mexico)
6   **Favourite book:** _The Idiot_ by Dostoyevsky (from Russia)
7   **Favourite fashion designer:** Yamamoto Yohji (from Japan)

1   My name_'s Carmina Moretti. I'm Italian._
2   My favourite food _is Kung Pao chicken. It's Chinese._
3   My favourite film _____ .
    _____ .
4   My favourite singer _____ .
    _____ .
5   My favourite actor _____ .
    _____ .
6   My favourite book _____ .
    _____ .
7   My favourite fashion designer _____ .
    _____ .

Pronunciation | syllable stress

4 **a** 🔊 05 Listen to the words from the box and complete the table.

> ~~American~~   Brazilian   ~~British~~   Chinese
> German   ~~Indian~~   Italian   Japanese
> Mexican   Polish   Russian   Spanish

1	oOoo	American, _____ , _____
2	Oo	British, _____ , _____ , _____ , _____
3	Ooo	Indian, _____
4	oO	_____
5	ooO	_____

b Listen again and say the words.

Grammar | possessive adjectives: *my, your, his* and *her*

5 Complete the dialogues with *my, your, his* or *her*.

A: Is she Polish?
B: Yes, she is.
A: What's *her* name?
B: Magda.

1 A: Is he Spanish?
   B: Yes, he is.
   A: What's ____ name?
   B: Rafael.

2 A: Are you Mexican?
   B: No, I'm not. I'm from the USA.
   A: What's ____ name?
   B: ____ name's Ross.

3 A: Who's she?
   B: ____ name's Tamsin Brett.
   A: Is she ____ favourite singer?
   B: Yes, she is.

4 A: Who's he?
   B: ____ name's Trey Parker. He's American.
   A: Is he ____ favourite actor?
   B: No, he isn't.

6 Correct the mistakes.

It's a my car.

It's my car.

1 What's he's name?

   _____

2 His my favourite singer.

   _____

3 Who's hers favourite actor?

   _____

4 What's you're favourite food?

   _____

5 Her name Ibis.

   _____

6 Your British.

   _____

7 Look at the information and complete the text with *I'm, my, you, your, he's, his, she's* or *her*.

Name:	Victor
From:	the UK
Favourite film:	*Singing in the Rain*
Favourite book:	*Animal Farm*

Name:	Alice
From:	the USA
Favourite film:	*Titanic*
Favourite book:	*The Great Gatsby*

Name:	Thiago
From:	Brazil
Favourite film:	*La Strada*
Favourite book:	*The Alchemist*

What's your name?
Victor: *My* name's Victor. *She's* Alice and
(1) _____ name is Thiago.

Where are (2) _____ from?
Victor: (3) _____ British, (4) _____ American
and (5) _____ Brazilian.

What is (6) _____ favourite film?
Victor: (7) _____ favourite film is Singing in the
Rain with Gene Kelly. It's a classic American
film. (8) _____ favourite film is La Strada.
It's a classic Italian film.
(9) _____ favourite is Titanic. Is Titanic
American?

What is her favourite book?
Victor: (10) _____ favourite book is The Great
Gatsby by F Scott Fitzgerald. (11) _____
favourite is Animal Farm by George Orwell
and (12) _____ favourite is The Alchemist
by Paolo Coelho. Coelho is Brazilian.

2 My life

Vocabulary | family

1 Match the opposites.

	Female		Male
1	mother	a	son
2	sister	b	husband
3	daughter	c	grandfather
4	grandmother	d	boyfriend
5	wife	e	father
6	aunt	f	brother
7	girlfriend	g	uncle

Vocabulary | the alphabet

2 **a** 06 Listen to the letters. Match the vowel sounds of the letters (a–z) with the vowel sounds of the words (1–7).

**a b c d e f g h i j k l m
n o p q r s t u v w x y z**

1 **n<u>a</u>me** /eɪ/
_a_, ___, ___, ___

2 **sh<u>e</u>** /iː/
_b_, _c_, ___, ___, ___, ___, ___, ___

3 **t<u>e</u>n** /e/
_f_, _l_, ___, ___, ___, ___

4 **m<u>y</u>** /əɪ/
_i_, ___

5 **z<u>e</u>ro** /əʊ/
___

6 **wh<u>o</u>** /uː/
_q_, ___, ___

7 **<u>are</u>** /ɑː/
___

b Listen again and say the letters.

Listening

3 07 Cover the audioscript. Listen and complete the information on the cards.

①

Fast Fit Gym
Name: Stefania Giordano
Membership: Gold
Membership Number: (1) _ _ _ _ _ _ _ _ _

②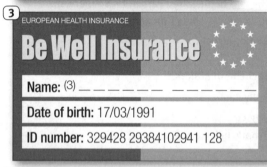

Hi-Rate CREDIT CARD
7842 0293 3293 1738
Mr (2) _ _ _ _   _ _ _ _ _ _ _

③

EUROPEAN HEALTH INSURANCE
Be Well Insurance
Name: (3) _ _ _ _ _ _ _   _ _ _ _ _ _
Date of birth: 17/03/1991
ID number: 329428 29384102941 128

AUDIOSCRIPT

1
A: Hello. What's your name, please?
B: My name's Stefania Giordano.
A: How do you spell Giordano, please.
B: G - I - O - R - D - A - N - O.
A: And what's your membership number?
B: It's A - L - 7 - 9 - 6 - S - C - K.
A: OK. Thank you. How can I help?

2
A: OK, what's your name, please?
B: It's Ian Evering.
A: Can you spell that, please.
B: Yes. Ian: I - A - N. And Evering: E - V - E - R - I - N - G.
A: Thank you very much.

3
A: What's your name, please?
B: Leslie Knight.
A: Can you spell that, please?
B: Yes. L - E - S - L - I - E and Knight is K - N - I - G - H - T.
A: Thank you.

How to... | introduce a friend

4 Put the words in the correct order to make dialogues.

1 A: is Jon. this Alan,

Alan, this _____

B: you, meet Jon. to Nice

_____

C: meet too, Nice Alan. to you

_____

2 A: is Roni. Elif, this

Elif, _____

B: to you, Roni. meet Nice

_____

C: too, to Elif. meet Nice you,

_____

Grammar 1 | *to be*: *you* (plural), *we* and *they*

5 Rewrite the dialogues with the words in brackets.

A: Is she married? (they)

B: Yes, she is.

A: *Are they married?*

B: *Yes, they are.*

1 A: He is Polish. (they)

B: Where is he from in Poland?

A: _____

B: _____

2 A: Am I late? (we)

B: No, you aren't.

A: _____

B: _____

3 A: Where is she from? (they)

B: She's from Brazil.

A: _____

B: _____

4 A: I'm not Spanish, I'm Italian (we).

B: Are you from Rome?

A: _____

B: _____

6 Read the dialogues. Correct the mistakes.

A: Where are Mum and Dad? ✓

B: They in the garden with Aunt Bea. *'re*

1 A: Are Yanni and Petra married? ___

B: No, they are. They're friends. ___

2 A: Is you and your wife from Moscow? ___

B: No, we aren't. Alina's from St Petersburg and I'm from Kazan. ___

3 A: Your friends are in the garden. ___

B: They not my friends. They're Erica's friends. ___

4 A: Hello. Who is you? ___

B: I'm Francesca and this is my husband, Tony. We're from Canada. ___

Grammar 2 | possessive adjectives: *our*, *your* and *their*

7 Circle the correct word.

My name is Kelly and his name is Larry. (We're)/Our from Liverpool.

1 *They're/Their* daughter is Lucy.

2 Richard and Julia are British. *They're/Their* my friends.

3 Hello, Mr and Mrs Smith. Where is *you're/your* daughter?

4 Hello, Mr and Mrs Brown. *You're/Your* in room twenty-one.

5 *We're/Our* car is very old.

6 What's *they're/their* email address?

7 Julian is a singer but *we're/our* actors.

8 Complete the email with *we're*, *you're*, *they're*, *our*, *your* or *their*.

From:	rebeccaclark55@talkmail.com
To:	tomandsusan.clark@squeedle.co.uk
Subject:	We're in Recife!
Attachments:	family.jpg

Hi Mum and Dad,

How are you? Sarah and I are fine. *We're* in Recife in Brazil. (1) _____ hotel is great and (2) _____ in room 888!

Belinda and Cipriano are in Recife too. They're (3) _____ friends and (4) _____ from São Paulo.

The attachment is a photo of Belinda, Cipriano and Carlita in (5) _____ house in São Paulo. It's big! Carlita is (6) _____ daughter. She's beautiful.

Love,

Rebecca

P.S Thanks for (7) _____ email!

Vocabulary | personal objects

1 Complete the crossword.

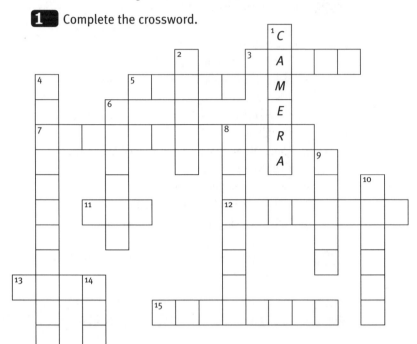

Pronunciation | /æ/ and /e/

2 **a** 🔘 o8 Listen to the words from the box and complete the table. Use the underlined sound.

| apple bag café camera |
| friend grandpa Internet pen |
| seven taxi umbrella |

/æ/	/e/
apple	friend
————	————
————	————
————	————
————	————

b Listen again and say the words.

ACROSS

DOWN

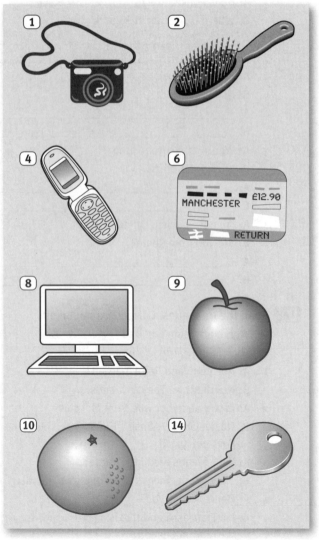

Grammar | *a/an* and noun plurals

3 Answer the questions with *a/an*.

What is it?

It's a key.

What is it?

_____ .

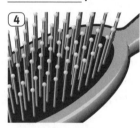

What is it?

_____ .

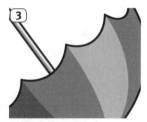

What is it?

_____ .

What is it?

_____ .

What is it?

_____ .

4 Write dialogues with the prompts. Use plural nouns.

Woman: (purse) *Are they purses?*

Man: (camera) *No. They aren't purses. They're cameras.*

1 Woman: (television) _____
_____ ?

  Man: (computer) _____
_____ .

2 Woman: (mobile phone) _____
_____ ?

  Man: (iPod) _____
_____ .

3 Woman: (watch) _____
_____ ?

  Man: (mobile phone) _____
_____ .

Listening

5 🔘 09 Cover the audioscript. Listen. What is in Leo's bag? What is in Charlie's bag? Complete the lists.

Leo

two mobile phones

1 _____

2 _____

3 _____

Charlie

4 _____

5 _____

6 _____

7 _____

8 _____

AUDIOSCRIPT

Leo

Int: Hello, Sir.

Leo: Oh, hello.

Int: What's your name?

Leo: My name's Leo.

Int: What's in your bag, Leo?

Leo: What's in my bag? Oh, er ... well a mobile phone. No, no, two mobile phones ...

Int: Two?

Leo: Yes, one is my phone and one is a work phone.

Int: OK.

Leo: And an umbrella, and a book. Oh, no. My book is at home. Um ... a brush and ... er ... two apples. That's it!

Int: OK, great. Thank you very much.

Charlie

Int: Hello, Madam.

Charlie: Hello.

Int: What's your name?

Charlie: I'm Charlie.

Int: What's in your bag, Charlie?

Charlie: Well ... my passport and ... a camera and three books. No. Not three books. Four books!

Int: Four books!

Charlie: Yes. For my holiday. And ... a brush. No, Two brushes and my purse. That's it.

Int: OK, great. Thank you very much.

Vocabulary | numbers 11–101

1 Match the numbers (1–10) with the numbers (a–j).

1	fifty-one		a	93
2	forty-eight		b	15
3	eleven		c	73
4	sixteen		d	48
5	ninety-three		e	11
6	seventy-three		f	51
7	fifteen		g	84
8	sixty		h	39
9	eighty-four		i	60
10	thirty-nine		j	16

2 Write the next two numbers.

two   four   eight   sixteen
thirty-two   sixty-four _____

1 eleven   twenty-two   thirty-three   forty-four

_____

2 ninety   eighty   seventy   sixty

_____

3 sixteen   fifteen   fourteen   thirteen

_____

4 forty-nine   fifty-six   sixty-three   seventy

_____

5 twenty-seven   thirty-six   forty-five

_____

6 sixteen   twenty-five   thirty-six   forty-nine

_____

7 ninety   ten   eighty   twenty

_____

Pronunciation | saying numbers

3 🔘 10 Listen and write the numbers you hear.

_14_

a ____
b ____
c ____
d ____
e ____
f ____
g ____
h ____
i ____

How to... | ask and talk about age

4 Write the dialogues. Use the prompts

Jane/19

A: *How old is she?*
B: *She's nineteen.*

1 Bob/52
   A: _____
   B: _____

2 you/21
   A: _____
   B: _____

3 Jenny and Tim/11 and 12
   A: _____
   B: _____

4 you and your sister/30
   A: _____
   B: _____

Grammar | *to be*: review

5 Make the sentences negative. Use the prompts.

A: I'm a teacher. (student)
B: *I'm not a teacher. I'm a student*

1 A: It's a camera. (iPod)
   B: _____
   _____

2 A: We're from the USA. (the UK)
   B: _____
   _____

3 A: Paris is my favourite country. (city)
   B: _____
   _____

4 A: He's my sister. (brother)
   B: _____
   _____

5 A: You're fifteen. (fifty)
   B: _____
   _____

6 A: They're friends. (cousins)
   B: _____
   _____

7 A: She's an accountant. (engineer)
   B: _____
   _____

6 **a** Complete the dialogues. Use contractions where possible.

1 **A:** Excuse me.
   B: Yes?
   A: _Are_ you from this town?
   B: Yes, we (1) _____ .
   A: Oh, good. Where (2) _____ Hotel Panorama?
   B: It (3) _____ over there.
   A: Thank you.

2 **A:** Hello, Madam. (4) _____ they your sons?
   A: He's my son but the other boy (5) _____ .
   B: How old (6) _____ they? (7) _____ they twelve?
   A: No, they (8) _____ . They (9) _____ ten.
   B: Sorry, Madam. The film is for children over twelve only.

3 **A:** Hello, Sir.
   B: Hello.
   A: (10) _____ they your bags?
   B: Yes, they (11) _____ .
   A: What (12) _____ your room number, Sir?
   B: It (13) _____ room 311.
   A: OK. Thank you, Sir.

b Match the dialogues (1–3) with the pictures (A–C).

Reading

7 Complete the family tree with the information about each person.

The Wallace family

He's Sam Wallace. His sister is Marie. He's forty-five years old. He's a teacher. His wife is Monica.

She's Patricia Wallace. Her son is Sam. She's sixty-eight years old. She's Italian.

He's Derek Wallace. His wife is Patricia and his daughter is Marie. He's sixty-five years old. He's American.

She's Monica Wallace. Her husband is Sam. She's forty-four years old. She's from France.

She's Marie Wallace. Her brother is Sam. She's thirty-eight years old. She's a doctor.

They're Malcolm and Debbie Wallace. They're twelve years old. His favourite sport is football and her favourite sport is basketball.

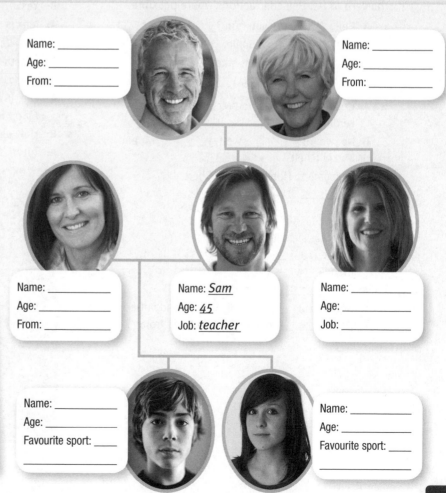

Name: _____
Age: _____
From: _____

Name: _____
Age: _____
From: _____

Name: _____
Age: _____
From: _____

Name: _Sam_
Age: _45_
Job: _teacher_

Name: _____
Age: _____
Job: _____

Name: _____
Age: _____
Favourite sport: _____
_____

Name: _____
Age: _____
Favourite sport: _____
_____

Grammar | to be

1 Choose the correct word or contraction.

He _____ from Russia.

a 'm   **b** 's   c 're

1 You _____ my friend.
   a 're   b 's   c 'm

2 We _____ sisters. We're cousins.
   a 'm not   b isn't   c aren't

3 Where _____ they from?
   a am   b is   c are

4 Who _____ she?
   a 's   b 'm   c 're

5 _____ they Polish?
   a Am   b Is   c Are

6 What _____ your phone number?
   a 'm   b 's   c 're

7 It _____ a phone. It's an iPod.
   a 'm not   b isn't   c aren't

8 Sylvia and I _____ married.
   a 'm not   b isn't   c aren't

9 Jenny is from the UK but I _____ .
   a 'm not   b isn't   c aren't

2 Complete the dialogues with the correct form of the verb *to be*. Use contractions where possible.

1 A: Hello. Where _are_ you from?
   B: I (1) _____ from Spain.
   A: (2) _____ you from Madrid?
   B: No, I (3) _____ . I (4) _____ from Jerez.

2 A: Hello. (5) _____ you Mr and Mrs Ferdinand?
   B: No, we (6) _____ . We (7) _____ Mr and Mrs Mitchell.
   A: Welcome to Hotel Franklin. Where (8) _____ your bags?
   B: They (9) _____ in the taxi.

3 A: (10) _____ he your brother?
   B: No, he (11) _____ . He (12) _____ my friend.
   A: (13) _____ he from the USA?
   B: No, he (14) _____ . His mother and father (15) _____ from the USA, but he's from Canada.

Possessive adjectives: *my, your, his, her, its, our, their*

3 Complete the sentences with the correct possessive adjective.

We're from Germany but _our_ parents are from Russia.

1 _____ name is Steven Jones. He's my cousin.

2 A: Hello. What's _____ name?
   B: I'm Tara White.

3 I'm Olivia and this is _____ husband, Greg.

4 Charles and Eva are our friends. _____ daughter is called Debbie.

5 The restaurant is called Homa. _____ food is Italian.

6 Julia and _____ mother are in London.

7 My husband and I are in the Bergman Hotel. _____ room is number 4-5-9.

4 Choose the correct word.

A: Who's she/her, in the photo. Is she (1) *you/your* sister?

B: No, she isn't. She's (2) *I/my* friend, Ellie.

A: How old is (3) *she/her*?

B: She's 24. (4) *She/Her* brother is Max.

A: Max Langley?

B: Yes!

A: Max is in (5) *I'm/my* English class.

B: Are Fitz and Marin in your class, too?

A: Yes, they are. (6) *They're/Their* brothers.

B: Are (7) *they/their*?

A: Yes. (8) *They're/Their* surname is Banica. Fitz and Marin Banica.

B: How old is Fitz?

A: (9) *He's/His* 23.

a/an and noun plurals

5 Complete each sentence with *a*, *an* or nothing (–).

Natalie is in – India.

1   Madrid is _____ great city.
2   He's my _____ brother.
3   It's _____ good film.
4   He's _____ actor.
5   What's your _____ email address?
6   Is it _____ orange?
7   Where is my _____ pen?
8   David is _____ English.
9   She's _____ singer.

6 Complete the dialogues with the plural form of the word in bold.

A: Is this your **pen**?
B: No. My *pens* are in my bag.

1   A: Is she your **sister**?
    B: No. My _____ are in Germany.
2   A: Where's your **brush**?
    B: My _____ are in my bag.
3   A: What's in your bag? A **watch** and a book?
    B: No. Two _____ and a book.
4   A: Is this your **camera**?
    B: No. My _____ are in my bag.
5   A: Where's my **orange**?
    B: Your _____ are here.

Vocabulary

7 Match 1–10 with a–j to make words.

1	foot	a	olate
2	stu	b	fé
3	pass	c	vision
4	sa	d	versity
5	doc	e	lice
6	uni	f	dent
7	ca	g	tor
8	tele	h	lad
9	po	i	ball
10	choc	j	port

8 Circle the correct word.

My *Spain* /*Spanish* passport is in my bag.

1   Are you from *the UK* /*British*?
2   My mother's *Italy* /*Italian*.
3   It's a *Russia* /*Russian* film.
4   Kyoto is in *Japan* /*Japanese*.
5   I'm *China* /*Chinese*.
6   Are they *France* /*French*?
7   It's an *USA* /*American* car.

9 Complete the words.

c a m e r a

1   p _ _ r s _ _
2   t _ _ c k _ _ t
3   b _ _ _ k
4   _ p p l _ _
5   m _ b _ l _ p h _ n _ _
6   _ _ m b r _ _ l l a
7   _ _ r _ n g _ _
8   b _ _ s _ n _ _ s s   c _ _ r d
9   c _ _ m p _ _ t _ _ r

10 Write the number in full.

84   *eighty-four*

1   79   _____
2   23   _____
3   13   _____
4   8   _____
5   101 _____
6   12   _____
7   57   _____
8   15   _____
9   30   _____

11 Complete the sentences for Ellen.

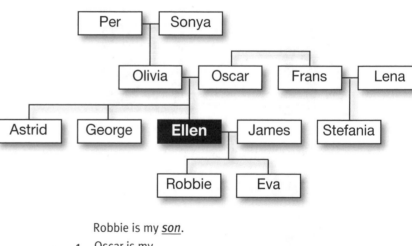

Robbie is my *son*.

1   Oscar is my _____ .
2   Stefania is my _____ .
3   Astrid is my _____ .
4   Eva is my _____ .
5   James is my _____ .
6   Sonya is my _____ .
7   George is my _____ .
8   Per is my _____ .
9   Olivia is my _____ .
10 Frans is my _____ .
11 Lena is my _____ .

Vocabulary | places in town

1 Complete the puzzle. Find the hidden UK city.

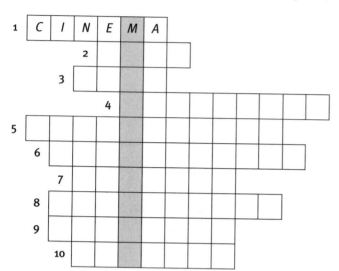

1	C	I	N	E	M	A

2
3
4
5
6
7
8
9
10

Grammar | possessive 's: singular and plural

2 Look at the table and write sentences.

	Luka	Sandra
parents	from Italy	from Brazil
children	daughter = 3 son = 5	sons = 12 and 15
favourite food and drink	favourite food = sushi	favourite drink = coffee

(sushi)   *Luka's favourite food is sushi.*
(Brazil)   *Sandra's parents are from Brazil.*

1   (from Italy) _____

_____

2   (coffee) _____

_____

3   (three and five) _____

_____

4   (twelve and fifteen) _____

_____

3 Write questions and answers. Use the prompts.
Laura/favourite snack
pizza
A: *What's Laura's favourite snack?*
B: *It's pizza.*

1   Grace/parents
   from Argentina
   A: _____
   B: _____

2   Leo/surname
   Webber
   A: _____
   B: _____

3   Elif/parents
   from Turkey
   A: _____
   B: _____

4   Valentina/best friend
   Catalina
   A: _____
   B: _____

5   Sem/children
   three and five
   A: _____
   B: _____

4 Put the apostrophe in the correct place.

My parents' holiday house is in Cape Cod.

1 What is your sisters favourite snack?
2 What is Vladimirs surname?
3 My childs favourite food is cheese.
4 Her childrens favourite food is chocolate.
5 That's my mothers favourite film.

5 Read the sentences. What is the meaning of 's in each sentence? Write P (possessive 's) or I (*is*).

Armando's my brother. _I_

1 Bianca's brother is Claudio. ___
2 Where is Keiko's bag? ___
3 Johann's not here today. ___
4 Who is Hilda's friend? ___
5 Jake's camera is great. ___
6 Karla's my friend. ___
7 Is Suzanne's surname Webb? ___

Vocabulary | snacks and drinks

6 Look at the pictures. Complete the receipts.

(1)

a A Chicken sandwich   £2.99

b A _____   £1.49

c A sparkling _____   £0.99

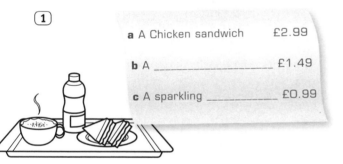

(2)

a A Turkish _____   €0.99

b A cheese _____   €3.99

c An orange _____   €1.20

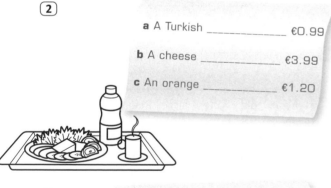

(3)

a A prawn _____ $2.89

b A piece of _____ _____ $1.79

c A cup of _____ $1.10

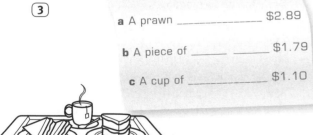

Pronunciation | /ɒ/

7 **a** Which words contain the /ɒ/ sound?

	a	b	c
	a prawn	b name	c what
1	a doctor	b actor	c singer
2	a cake	b chocolate	c roll
3	a coffee	b tea	c water
4	a cheese	b not	c sugar
5	a café	b snack	c shop
6	a Jane	b Jon	c James
7	a orange	b apple	c cheese

b 🔘 11 Listen and check.

How to... | order food and drink

8 Complete the dialogue.

A: Can I _help_ you?
B: Yes. Can I (1) _____ a cheese sandwich, please?
A: Eat in or take (2) _____ ?
B: Eat in, please.
A: Sure. Anything (3) _____ ?
B: Yes. A coffee, (4) _____ .
A: With milk and (5) _____ ?
B: Milk, please. (6) _____ sugar.

Vocabulary | adjectives

1 Find eight more adjectives in the word square.

N	S	L	D	Y	N	C	Z	P
I	C	L	O	S	E	D	X	H
C	S	M	T	B	F	R	E	T
E	J	K	C	O	L	D	H	O
O	J	L	H	I	E	V	D	P
E	X	P	E	N	S	I	V	E
O	Y	B	A	D	U	P	W	N
F	R	U	P	S	M	A	L	L
G	W	G	D	G	O	O	D	Y

2 **a** Choose the correct adjective for each photo.

hot ⟨old⟩ free

1 cheap big closed

2 expensive slow free

3 cold fast big

4 nice small closed

5 hot cold slow

b Write the opposite of each answer in exercise 2a.

old – new

1 _____
2 _____
3 _____
4 _____
5 _____

3 Complete the sentences with the words from the box.

> fresh old cold nice free ~~cheap~~ fast open

This mobile phone is only €9.99. That's really *cheap*.

1 I'm sorry, this shop is closed now. We're _____ again tomorrow morning.
2 My coffee isn't very hot. Is your coffee _____ , too?
3 Frans is an _____ friend from school.
4 My old computer is really slow. How much is a new, _____ computer?
5 This car park isn't _____ . It's $2 for one hour.
6 These cakes aren't _____ . They're two days old.
7 **A:** Is your hotel room good?
   B: Yes, it's very _____ .

Pronunciation | /əʊ/

4 **a** Underline the /əʊ/ sounds in these sentences.

It's not <u>o</u>pen. It's cl<u>o</u>sed.

1 Hello. Is this Joe's hotel?

2 So, is this your clothes shop?

3 Oh, no! My computer is so slow.

b 🔵 12 Listen and check. Then say the sentences.

Grammar | position of adjectives

5 Put the words in the correct order to make questions and sentences.

a new./computer/The/is

The computer is new.

b computer./a/new/It's

It's a new computer.

1 a salad/Is/good?/your

_____

b good/a/Is/it/salad?

_____

2 a sandwiches/the/Are/fresh?

_____

b fresh/Are/sandwiches?/they

_____

3 a is/Her/expensive./phone

_____

b an/phone./It's/expensive

_____

4 a nice/apples./They/are

_____

b nice./apples/The/are

_____

6 Correct the mistakes.

Is he your boyfriend new?

Is he your new boyfriend?

1 The shoe shop closed is.

_____

2 This salad is nice really.

_____

3 Can I have a piece big of chocolate cake?

_____

4 Small your sandwiches are.

_____

5 They expensive aren't.

_____

6 It's very nice deli.

_____

7 That's really expensive car.

_____

Reading

7 Read the text and answer the questions.

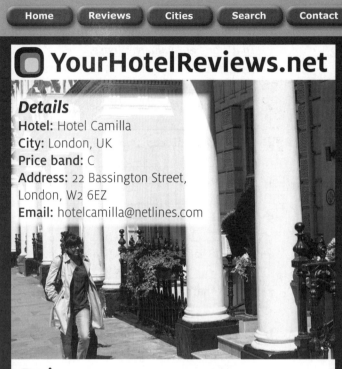

Home **Reviews** **Cities** **Search** **Contact**

⬤ YourHotelReviews.net

Details
Hotel: Hotel Camilla
City: London, UK
Price band: C
Address: 22 Bassington Street, London, W2 6EZ
Email: hotelcamilla@netlines.com

Review

My favourite hotel is in London. It's called Hotel Camilla and it's on Bassington Street, near the centre of town. It's a small hotel – about ten rooms – but it isn't very expensive and it's very good. The white sheets in the rooms are from Italy, the flowers are fresh every day and the food and drink in each room is free.

The managers of Hotel Camilla are Luis and his wife, Camilla. Luis is Spanish and Camilla is British. The guests are from all over the world. Rooms are about £80 for one night – that's cheap in London!

Emmanuela, Italy

What is the name of the hotel?

It's called Hotel Camilla.

1 Where is it?

_____

2 Is the hotel big?

_____

3 Where are the sheets from?

_____

4 How much is the food and drink in the rooms?

_____

5 Who are the managers of the hotel?

_____

6 Which country are they from?

_____

7 How much is a room at the hotel?

_____

Vocabulary | prices

1 **a** Correct the mistakes.

(€1.90) That one euro ninety, please.

That's one euro ninety, please.

1 ($2.45) That's two dollar forty-five, please.

_____ .

2 (€0.50) That's fifty pence, please.

_____ .

3 (£6.29) That's six euros twenty-nine, please.

_____ .

4 (€3.60) That's three euro sixty cents, please.

_____ .

5 ($0.99) That's ninety-nine dollars, please.

_____ .

6 (€11.49) That's eleven forty-nine euros, please.

_____ .

7 (£0.80) That's eighty pounds, please.

_____ .

b Look at the pictures. Complete the sentences.

The CDs *are nine pounds eighty-nine*.

1 The shoes _____ .

2 The camera _____ .

3 The bag _____ .

4 The books _____ .

5 The mobile phone _____ .

How to... | ask for prices and pay for things

2 **a** Complete the dialogues.

1 A: How *much* is that?

B: (1) _____ €10.99, please.

A: (2) _____ you are.

B: Thank you. (3) _____ your change.

A: Thank you.

2 A: How much is that (4) _____ ?

B: (5) _____ $2.20, please.

A: Can I (6) _____ by card?

B: Yes. Enter your PIN (7) _____ , please. Here's your card and your receipt.

A: Thank you.

b Write a dialogue. Use the prompts.

A: (How/that?)   *How much is that?*

B: (£3.50)   (1) _____ .

A: (pay/card?)   (2) _____ ?

B: (Sure/PIN number)   (3) _____ .

A: OK.

B: (card/receipt)   (4) _____ .

A: Thank you.

Grammar | this, that, these, those

3 Choose the correct sentence for each picture.

(a) Is this your mobile phone?

b Is that your mobile phone?

c Is those your mobile phone?

a That's the gallery.

b These is the gallery.

c Those is the gallery.

a Is this your shoes?

b Are these your shoes?

c Are those your shoes?

4 Put the words in the correct order to make sentences.

are   These   nice.   flowers
These flowers are nice.

1 €24.   bag   That   is

_____

2 suitcase?   your   Is   this

_____

3 those   Are   new?   shoes

_____

4 closed   shops   today.   are   These

_____

5 Clive.   This   my   is   brother,

_____

6 are   Those   expensive.   chocolates

_____

7 How   computer?   much   that   is

_____

Vocabulary | colours

5 Complete the colours.

b r **o w n**
1 w h _ _ _   4 b _ _ e
2 o r _ _ _ _ _   5 b l _ _ _ _
3 g r _ _ _ _   6 y e _ _ _ _ _
                      7 r _ _

6 Look at the flags. What are the correct colours?

Italy

1 Spain

The Italian flag is green, white and red.

_____ .

2 Argentina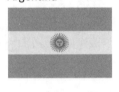

3 Poland

_____ .

_____ .

4 Germany

5 Brazil

_____ .

_____ .

Listening

7 🔊 13 Cover the audioscripts and listen. Complete the table for each dialogue.

	Dialogue 1	Dialogue 2	Dialogue 3
buy	1 *a black purse*	4	7
price	2	5	8
cash/card	3	6	9

AUDIOSCRIPT

1
A: Can I help you?
B: Yes. How much are those black purses?
A: They're fourteen Euros ninety-nine. And those white ones are twelve ninety-nine.
B: Oh, OK, er …
A: They're really nice purses.
B: Yes, er … can I have a black purse?
A: Certainly. That's fourteen ninety-nine, please.
B: Can I pay by card?
A: Sure. Just enter your PIN number here. Thank you. Here's your purse and your receipt. Thank you.
B: Thanks very much. Bye.

2
A: How much are the apples?
B: These green apples are one pound ninety-nine a kilo and those red apples are two pounds nine pence a kilo.
A: Can I have two kilos of green apples, please?
B: Certainly. It's a bit over. Is that OK?
A: Yes, that's fine.
B: That's four pounds twenty, please.
A: Here you are.
B: Thank you. And here's your change.
A: Thanks. Bye.

3
A: Can I help you?
B: Yes. How much is this black camera?
A: That's eighty-nine dollars ninety-nine.
B: Eighty-nine ninety-nine. Phew! That's expensive.
A: This blue camera is only fifty-five dollars ninety-nine. It's really nice.
B: Oh, yes. It's nice. Can I pay by card?
A: Of course.
B: Great. OK. Can I have the blue camera, then?

4 Travel

Vocabulary | places

1 a Add the missing letter to each word.

palac   _palace_

1   airpot   _____
2   galery   _____
3   musum   _____
4   rivr   _____
5   thetre   _____
6   natonal park   _____
7   the se   _____
8   bech   _____
9   lak   _____
10   maket   _____
11   montain   _____

b Match the pictures with the words from exercise 1a.

palace

_____

_____

_____

_____

_____

Vocabulary | adjectives of opinion

2 a Circle the correct adjective.

★★★★★
(fantastic)/terrible

1   ★★★★☆
not bad/nice

2   ★★★☆☆
OK/awful

3   ★★☆☆☆
not very good/great

4   ★☆☆☆☆
awful/not bad

b Complete the sentences with the words from the box.

| good   fantastic   OK   ~~not very good~~   terrible |

He's not very good.

1 _____

2 _____

3 _____

4 _____

How to... | give an opinion

3 Put the words in the correct order to make sentences.

is/think/this/beautiful./I/beach

I think this beach is beautiful.

sea/clean./very/think/don't/is/I/the

I don't think the sea is very clean.

1 city./I/New York/great/think/a/is

_____

2 think/I/good./shops/those/are/don't/very

_____

3 friend./Francis/is/think/best/I/my

_____

4 the/think/expensive./don't/market/I/is/very

_____

Grammar | *there is/are; some; a lot of*

4 Complete the sentences with *there's* or *there are*.

A Quick Guide to Five English Towns

Brighton

Brighton is only one hour from London. There's a beach and (1) ____ nice shops and cafés.

Canterbury

Canterbury is in the south-east of England. It's about ten kilometres from the sea. (2) ____ a famous cathedral and (3) ____ a beautiful river – the River Stour.

Nottingham

Nottingham is in the centre of England. (4) ____ good shops and restaurants and (5) ____ a castle near the centre of town. (6) ____ also a museum about Robin Hood.

York

York is about ninety kilometres from Manchester. It's an old city and (7) ____ streets from the 1400s. (8) ____ also a top university, a river and a famous cathedral – York Minster.

Bristol

Bristol is in the west of England. (9) ____ a beautiful bridge by Isambard Kingdom Brunel – the Clifton Suspension Bridge. (10) ____ also great museums and galleries.

5 Replace the words in **bold** with *some* or *a lot of*.

There are **over 12,000** McDonald's restaurants in the USA. *a lot of*

1 There are **three** big museums in South Kensington, London. _____
2 There are **over 250** castles in Scotland. _____
3 There are **about 70** markets in Paris. _____
4 There are **six** big rivers in Switzerland. _____
5 There are **three** important film studios in Moscow. _____

6 Complete the text. Use *there's* or *there are* and the prompts in brackets.

Home | Gallery | Trips & Tips | Contact | Link

Travel tips: Vancouver

Vancouver in Canada is a fantastic city. It is number one on a list of best cities to live in. But is it a good city for tourists? Write your comments below.

Comments

There are a lot of (a lot) galleries in downtown Vancouver. They are great for tourists.
Billy Coe, Los Angeles

(1) ____ (some) nice museums in Vancouver. (2) ____ (a) science museum and a maritime museum. The Museum of Vancouver is also great.
Jenny Carthy, Toronto

The shops in Vancouver are really good. (3) ____ (a lot) shopping malls and (4) ____ (also/a lot) small shops. (5) ____ (some) nice shops on Main Street with things from local designers.
Ahmet Wallace, New York

The restaurants in Vancouver are great. (6) ____ (about 100) Chinese restaurants and 150 Japanese restaurants.
Lee Yamamoto, Tokyo

(7) ____ (a) film festival in September – it's fantastic. (8) ____ (some) other arts festivals in Vancouver. They're really good, too.
Yolanda Cerdá, Madrid

Vocabulary | prepositions of place

1 Find the prepositions of place from the box in the word square.

> in front of   in   near   next to   on   opposite
> under

	A	G	B	U	R	F	S
I	A	G	B	U	R	F	S
N	E	X	T	T	O	D	U
F	X	U	N	L	O	O	N
R	C	O	N	Z	A	H	D
O	P	P	O	S	I	T	E
N	M	P	J	S	N	Y	R
T	Q	N	E	A	R	U	H
O	A	L	K	D	G	M	B
F	D	G	E	K	I	Y	W

2 Look at the picture. Complete the sentences with a preposition of place from the box.

> in front of   opposite   next to   near   under

The man is _in_ the café.

1 The café is _____ the bookshop.
2 The bus stop is _____ the café.
3 The bookshop is _____ the restaurant.
4 The bank is _____ the café.
5 The woman is _____ the bookshop.

Grammar | *there isn't/aren't; is/are there ... ?; any*

3 Look at the shopping centre plan below. Complete the questions and answers.

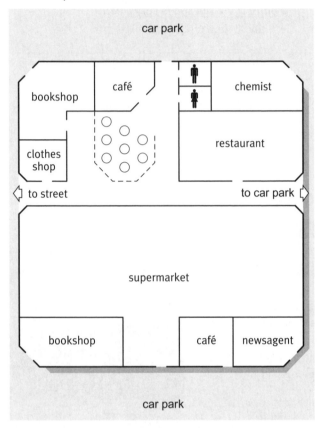

(chemist)
A: *Is there a chemist in this shopping centre?*
B: *Yes, there is.*
(banks)
A: *Are there any banks in this shopping centre?*
B: *No, there aren' t.*
1 (cinema)
  A: _____
  B: _____
2 (shoe shops)
  A: _____
  B: _____
3 (bookshops)
  A: _____
  B: _____
4 (car park)
  A: _____
  B: _____

4 Write affirmative or negative sentences about the shopping centre in Exercise 3.

There's a car park. (car park)

There aren't any galleries. (galleries)

1 _____ . (restaurant)
2 _____ . (supermarket)
3 _____ . (shoe shops)
4 _____ . (train station)
5 _____ . (bookshops)
6 _____ . (museums)
7 _____ . (clothes shop)
8 _____ . (cinema)

How to... | ask where a place is

5 Complete the dialogues with the correct word.

1 **A:** Excuse me, is *there* a supermarket (1) _____ here?
   B: No, (2) _____ isn't.

2 **A:** (3) _____ me, is the Science Museum near here?
   B: Yes, it (4) _____ . It's opposite the train station.

3 **A:** (5) _____ there any cafés or restaurants near this hotel?
   B: Yes, there (6) _____ . There are two restaurants on West Street.
   A: Great. (7) _____ you.
   B: You're (8) _____ .

4 **A:** Excuse me. (9) _____ there a toilet in this station?
   B: No, sorry, (10) _____ isn't.

Pronunciation | /θ/ and /ð/

6 a How is 'th' pronounced in the words below? Tick (✓) the correct column.

	/θ/	/ð/
think	✓	☐
this	☐	✓
1 that	☐	☐
2 three	☐	☐
3 mother	☐	☐
4 these	☐	☐
5 thirty	☐	☐
6 thank	☐	☐
7 there	☐	☐
8 theatre	☐	☐
9 those	☐	☐
10 brother	☐	☐
11 they	☐	☐

b 🔊 14 Listen and check.

c 🔊 15 Say the sentences. Then listen, check and repeat.

1 I think there's a theatre over there.
2 These cameras are cheap. They're thirty-three per cent off.
3 My mother and brother are in that café over there.

Listening

7 🔊 16 Listen and complete the questions below.

A: *Is there a hotel near here?*
B: Yes, there are two. There's a big hotel opposite the train station and there's a very nice hotel next to the cinema on Venice Road.
A: Great, thanks.

1 **A:** Excuse me. (1) _____ ?
   B: Err ... no, there aren't.
   A: Oh no!
   B: Sorry.
   A: Never mind.

2 **A:** Excuse me. (2) _____ ?
   B: Yes, there is. There's one opposite the supermarket.
   A: Great. Thank you.
   B: You're welcome.

3 **A:** Excuse me. (3) _____ ?
   B: Yes, there are. There's a café on Carnival Street, next to the supermarket. And there's a restaurant opposite the cinema.
   A: Thank you!

8 Listen again and complete the map below.

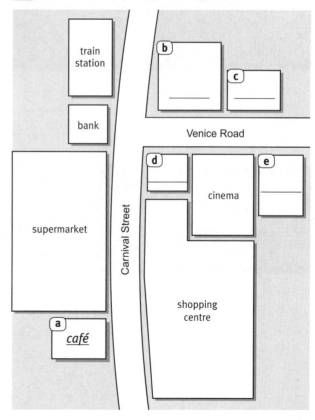

Vocabulary | telling the time

1 Write the time next to each clock.

ten o' clock   *quarter to five*   1 _____   2 _____   3 _____

4 _____   5 _____   6 _____   7 _____   8 _____

2 Look at the departure boards and write dialogues. Use the prompts.

DEPARTURES		TIME NOW: 14:15	
TIME	DESTINATION	EXPECTED	PLATFORM
14.25	PISA CENTRALE	ON TIME	1

A: *Excuse me. What's the time, please?*
B: *It's quarter past two.*
A: *And what time is the train to Pisa Centrale?*
B: *It's at twenty-five past two.*

1

DEPARTURES		TIME NOW: 19:20	
TIME	DESTINATION	EXPECTED	PLATFORM
19.35	IZMIT	ON TIME	2

A: _____
B: _____
A: _____
B: _____

2

DEPARTURES		TIME NOW: 09:55	
TIME	DESTINATION	EXPECTED	PLATFORM
10.30	KAZAN	ON TIME	14

A: _____
B: _____
A: _____
B: _____

Listening

3 🔘 17 Cover the audioscript. Listen and write the times you hear.

5:45

1 _____
2 _____
3 _____
4 _____

AUDIOSCRIPT

A: Excuse me. What's the time, please?
B: Let me see. Er ... it's quarter to six.
A: That's great. Thank you.

1 A: Excuse me. What's the time, please?
  B: It's half three.
  A: Thanks.
  B: You're welcome.

2 A: Sally, what's the time?
  B: It's twenty to two.
  A: Twenty to two? Ok. Thanks.

3 A: Excuse me. What's the time, please?
  B: Er ... It's ten past ten.
  A: Thank you.
  B: You're welcome.

4 A: What's the time, Henry?
  B: It's twenty-five to eight.
  A: Thanks.

How to... | buy a train ticket

4 **a** Complete the dialogue. One word is missing from each line of the dialogue.

A: Can I a return to Liverpool Central Station, please?

*Can I **have** a return to Liverpool Central station, please?*

B: Is £13.50, please.

(1) _____

A: Here are.

(2) _____

B: Thank.

(3) _____

A: What is the next train?

(4) _____

B: It at 10:35.

(5) _____

A: And what platform is on?

(6) _____

B: Is on platform one.

(7) _____

b Cover the dialogue in Exercise 4a. Write a new dialogue. Use the prompts.

A: (single/Bergamo station) *Can I have a single to Bergamo station, please?*

B: (€5.10) _____

A: (Here) _____

B: (Thank) _____

A: (next train?) _____

B: (9:50) _____

A: (platform?) _____

B: (three) _____

Pronunciation | /ə/

5 **a** Underline the schwa /ə/ sound in each word.

gall<u>e</u>ry

1 theatre

2 river

3 under

4 opposite

5 London

6 station

b 18 Listen, check and repeat.

6 **a** How many schwa /ə/ sounds are in each sentence?

Th<u>e</u> th<u>ea</u>t<u>re</u> is opp<u>o</u>site th<u>e</u> gall<u>e</u>ry.   [5]

1 Is there a big river in London?   [ ]

2 What's the time? Is it seven o'clock?   [ ]

b Now say the sentences.

Reading

7 Read about three museums and complete the table.

name	National Railway Museum	Money Museum	Museum of Bad Art (MOBA)
city	*York*		
opening times			
cost			
there is/ are			

Three museums

The National Railway Museum in York, UK, is open from ten o'clock to six o'clock every day. It's five minutes walk from York station. There are over 100 trains in the museum and there's a lot of art. The museum is very good for children and there's a restaurant, a gift shop and a café. The museum is free, but the car park is £9 per day.

The Money Museum in Colorado Springs, USA, is open from half past ten to five o'clock. The museum is next to the Colorado Springs Fine Arts Centre. There are coins and paper money from all over the world. There is also an American dollar from 1804. The museum isn't very big, but there is a gift shop. It is $5 for adults.

The Museum of Bad Art (MOBA) in Dedham, near Boston, USA, is about twenty years old. It is in the basement of a theatre, next to the toilet. The museum is open from two o'clock to nine o'clock. There are over 400 pieces of bad art in the museum. Some of the art is really bad. There aren't any staff in the museum (it's very small) and there isn't a café, but there's a café upstairs in the theatre and the museum is free.

Review and consolidation 3–4

Possessive 's

1 Write questions. Use the prompts.

(What/Kieran/favourite film?)

What's Kieran's favourite film?

1 (Who/Fiona/sister?)

_____

2 (Where/the girls/passports?)

_____

3 (they/Oliver/shoes?)

_____

4 (What/Jennifer/email address?)

_____

5 (Where/your parents/bags?)

_____

6 (Who/Harvey/cousin?)

_____

7 (you/Leah/brother?)

_____

Position of adjectives

2 Choose the correct sentence.

a My bike is very slow. ✓

b My bike very slow is.

1 a Your iPod is small very.

b Your iPod is very small.

2 a Train tickets are really expensive.

b Train tickets are expensive really.

3 a Is the restaurant good?

b Is good the restaurant?

4 a Is it a shop new?

b Is it a new shop?

5 a Sorry, this shop closed.

b Sorry, this shop is closed.

this, that, these, those

3 Choose the correct word.

Those/This/These is my brother.

1 Who are *that/these/those* people opposite the restaurant?

2 How much is *that/these/those* hat?

3 Is *this/those/these* your camera?

4 *That/These/This* are my favourite shops.

5 Oh no! Where is *this/that/those* new book?

6 Can I have *those/these/that* white bag, please?

7 Are *that/these/this* shoes from Italy?

There is/are

4 Complete the dialogues with the correct form of *there is/are*.

1 A: Good morning. *Is there* a bank near here?

B: Yes, (1) _____ . It's on Paisley Street.

A: And (2) _____ any museums near here?

B: Yes, (3) _____ . (4) _____ a small museum on Baker Street and (5) _____ a big museum opposite the train station.

2 A: (6) _____ any good restaurants near here?

B: Yes, (7) _____ . (8) _____ a good Japanese restaurant on Gatson Street and (9) _____ two good Indian restaurants on Mile Road.

A: Great. And (10) _____ a cashpoint in this hotel?

B: No, (11) _____ . Sorry.

3 A: Good afternoon. (12) _____ any supermarkets near here?

B: No, (13) _____ .

A: (14) _____ a deli near here?

B: Yes, (15) _____ . It's next to the book shop.

some/a lot of/any

5 Read the dialogue. Choose the correct word or phrase.

A: Are there *some/any* nice cafés near here?

B: Yes, there are. There are (1) *some/any* nice cafés on Broad Street, near the market, and there are (2) *any/a lot of* cafés in the centre of town.

A: And what about restaurants? Are there (3) *some/any* good French restaurants near here?

B: There are (4) *a lot of/any* good Chinese restaurants near the centre, but there aren't (5) *some/any* French restaurants near here.

Vocabulary

6 Complete the dialogues with the words from the box.

> bus stop   ~~cashpoint~~   cheese sandwich   cold
> expensive   fantastic   gallery   purple

A: Excuse me. Is there a *cashpoint* near here?
B: Yes, there is. There's one in the bank over there.

1 A: Those blue shoes are really cheap.
  B: Cheap? No, they're really (1) _____ .

2 A: There's a new (2) _____ on Park Street.
  B: Is it good?
  A: Yes, it is. The art is really good.

3 A: Is that deli nice?
  B: Yes, it is. I think it's (3) _____ .

4 A: Is your coffee hot?
  B: No, it isn't. It's (4) _____ .

5 A: Can I help you?
  B: Yes. Can I have a (5) _____ and a cup of tea, please?

6 A: What colour is that umbrella?
  B: It's (6) _____ .

7 A: Excuse me. Is there a (7) _____ near here?
  B: Yes, there is. It's in front of the chemist on Fenton Street.

7 Match a price in A with a price in B.

A		B	
1	That's twelve forty-nine, please.	a	$2.99
2	That's twenty-two ninety-nine, please.	b	60¢
3	That's six nineteen, please.	c	€16.00
4	That's two ninety-nine, please.	d	$22.99
5	That's sixty-two, ninety-nine, please.	e	£20.90
6	That's sixteen euros, please.	f	£12.49
7	That's twenty pounds ninety, please.	g	€6.19
8	That's sixty cents, please.	h	£62.99

8 Choose the correct word for each picture.

 (on)/in/in front of

1 next to/in front of/opposite

2 near/in/under

3 in/on/near

4 next to/opposite/in front of

5 on/under/in

6 under/opposite/on

9 Write the time.

   It's quarter to four.

1 _____ .

2 _____ .

3 _____ .

4 _____ .

5 _____ .

6 _____ .

7 _____ .

8 _____ .

9 _____ .

5 People

Vocabulary | adjectives of appearance

1 **a** Find eight more adjectives of appearance in the word square.

F	Y	Y	O	U	N	G	O	E	L
A	E	N	V	D	J	F	A	I	R
D	A	N	C	X	E	A	R	W	D
A	T	T	R	A	C	T	I	V	E
R	A	G	J	V	P	G	E	R	T
M	A	A	E	B	S	L	I	M	T
C	L	H	I	Z	E	H	D	O	A
O	D	U	G	L	Y	B	V	E	L
L	B	S	H	O	R	T	R	E	L
D	F	M	T	H	I	N	N	B	K

b Label the pictures with opposite adjectives from Exercise 1a.

a *thin*   b *fat*

1   a _____   b _____

2   a _____   b _____

3   a _____   b _____

Vocabulary | *live, work, have* and *like*

2 Complete the dialogues with the words from the box.

> have   ~~like~~   live in   live with   work as   live
> work for   work in

A: Do you *like* New York?
B: Yes, I do. I love it.
1   A: Who do you _____ ?
    B: A big Spanish company.
2   A: Do you _____ alone?
    B: No, I don't.
3   A: Do you _____ an office?
    B: No, I don't.
4   A: Do you _____ any children?
    B: Yes, I do. I have a son and a daughter.
5   A: Do you _____ a small town?
    B: Yes, I do.
6   A: Do you _____ a teacher?
    B: No, I don't.
7   A: Who do you _____ ?
    B: My husband and my children.

Grammar | Present Simple: *I* and *you*

3 **a** Write sentences with *I like/I don't like*.
(☺ /cappuccino)
I like cappuccino.
(☹ /museums)
I don't like museums.
1   (☺ /rock music)
    _____
2   (☹ /football)
    _____
3   (☺ /computers)
    _____
4   (☹ /Indian food)
    _____
5   (☹ /James Bond films)
    _____
6   (☺ /children)
    _____

b Write questions and answers. Use the verbs given.

A: *Do you like* black coffee? (like)

B: Yes, *I do.*

1 A: _____ with your parents? (live)

B: No, _____ .

2 A: _____ any brothers or sisters? (have)

B: Yes, _____ .

3 A: _____ for a big company? (work)

B: No, _____ .

4 A: _____ in Mexico City? (live)

B: Yes, _____ .

5 A: _____ in a school? (work)

B: Yes, _____ .

Pronunciation | /uː/ and /əʊ/

4 a 🔘 19 Listen to the words from the box and match them with the sounds.

> ~~do~~   ~~don't~~   eur<u>o</u>   go   new   oh   so
> st<u>u</u>dents   those   two   who   you

1 /uː/   *do*, _____, _____, _____, _____, _____

2 /əʊ/   *don't*, _____, _____, _____, _____, _____

b Listen again and say the words.

5 a 🔘 20 Listen to the sentences below. How many times do you hear /uː/ and /əʊ/?

	/uː/	/əʊ/
Oh n<u>o</u>! D<u>o</u>n't go there.	0	4
1 What is there to do in Vancouver?	☐	☐
2 Those two new students are so nice.	☐	☐

b Say the sentences.

How to... | show interest

6 a Choose the correct words to complete each dialogue.

A: I have two children.

B: Really? That's *a shame /(great)*

1 A: I live in a very small house.

B: Really? That's *a shame / great!*

2 A: I don't live with my parents. I live with my friends.

B: Oh, I *see / do.*

b Write a response to each sentence.

A: I don't like this restaurant.

B: *Really? That's a shame.*

1 A: I don't work in Los Angeles. I work in San Francisco.

B: _____ .

2 A: I like my new job.

B: _____ .

Listening

7 a 🔘 21 Cover the audioscript and listen. What job does each man do?

b Listen again. Complete the conversation.

AUDIOSCRIPT

F.A.: Drink, Sir?

Larry: Yes, can I have an orange juice, please?

F.A.: And for you, Sir?

John: Can I (1) _____ a mineral water, please, sparkling. And an orange juice for my (2) _____ .

Larry: Thanks.

John: Thank you.

Larry: First time in New York?

John: (3) _____ ?

Larry: Is this your first time in New York?

John: Oh, no, it isn't. I (4) _____ a lot in New York. This is my wife, er ... she's asleep.

Larry: (5) _____ do you do?

John: I'm an actor. I work in theatres in London.

Larry: I see.

John: What do you (6) _____ ?

Larry: I work (7) _____ a big bank. Its offices are in the UK and the USA. I travel a lot.

John: Oh, I see. Where do you live?

Larry: I live in New York with my family. But a lot of the time I live in hotels ...

F.A. = Flight Attendant

Vocabulary | verbs of routine

1 **a** Choose the correct nouns to complete the verb phrases.

come
a work **b** shower **c** home (circled) **d** dinner
1 finish
a bed **b** TV **c** home **d** work
2 get
a work **b** up **c** shower **d** bed
3 go
a to bed **b** dinner **c** work **d** TV
4 have a
a up **b** dinner **c** home **d** shower
5 make
a shower **b** home **c** dinner **d** TV
6 start
a work **b** bed **c** home **d** shower
7 watch
a home **b** TV **c** up **d** bed

b Match the pictures with phrases from Exercise 1a.

10:30

10:45

_____get up_____ _____

11:30 17:00

_____ _____

18:00 02:30

_____ _____

Grammar | Present Simple: *he*, *she* and *it*

2 Write sentences for the pictures in Exercise 1b.
She gets up at 10:30.
1 _____
2 _____
3 _____
4 _____
5 _____

3 Make the positive sentences negative.
He likes chocolate.
He doesn't like chocolate.
1 William starts work early.
_____
2 He watches TV with his daughter.
_____
3 Irene has a shower every day.
_____
4 Ricky makes dinner for his children.
_____

4 Read the text and answer the questions.
Does Mrs Moody start work early? *Yes, she does.*
1 Does she have breakfast?
_____
2 Does she have a coffee in the morning?
_____
3 Does she go to the restaurant for lunch?
_____
4 Does she finish work late?
_____
5 Does she have any friends?
_____

Mrs Moody – the workaholic

My manager is called Mrs Moody. She's a workaholic. She starts work at seven o'clock every morning. She doesn't have breakfast. She has a coffee at eleven o'clock and she has salad for lunch. She doesn't go to the restaurant – she eats her salad at her desk. She finishes work at about eight o'clock. She doesn't have any friends.

Reading

5 **a** Read texts 1–3. Match the texts with the photos A–C.

1 Claudia loves clothes. She works on Saturdays but she doesn't work on Sundays or Mondays. She doesn't work in an office. Claudia has two children.

Claudia: *'I like my job. I start work at nine and finish at five. I have time for my children in the evening and on Sundays.'* _B_

2 Lin loves sports. She starts work late and she works in the evenings and at weekends. She doesn't work in a shop. She has a salad for lunch and pasta for dinner. She has a shower in the evening after work.

Lin: *'I love my job. I don't start work early and that's great. I hate early mornings!'* ____

3 Olivia works from Monday to Friday. She doesn't work at weekends. She starts work at nine and finishes at five every day. She doesn't work in a gym.

Olivia: *'My job is OK. I don't love it and I don't hate it. My manager is nice.'* ____

b Read the texts again. Complete the sentences with Claudia, Lin and Olivia.

Olivia doesn't work on Saturdays.

1 _____ works in a gym.
2 _____ doesn't start work at 9 o'clock every day.
3 _____ and _____ don't work in the evening.
4 _____ works in a shop.
5 _____ works in an office.
6 _____ and _____ like their jobs.

Pronunciation | /s/, /z/ and /ɪz/

6 **a** 22 Listen to the words from the box. How is the final *s* pronounced? Complete the table.

> ~~does~~ eats finishes gets goes likes
> lives starts watches

/s/	/z/	/ɪz/
_____	*does*	_____
_____	_____	_____
_____	_____	_____

b Listen again and say the words.

7 23 Say the sentences. Then listen and check.
1 My dad likes chicken.
2 What does she do?
3 He finishes work at one.
4 My sister eats chocolate for breakfast.
5 He lives alone.
6 Simon gets up at six.
7 Paula starts work at seven.
8 She watches a lot of TV.
9 He goes to bed at eleven.

Vocabulary | days of the week

1 **a** Complete the days of the week. Then put them in order.

W e d n e s day __
Th _ _ _ day __
F _ _ day __
M _ _ day _1_
S _ t _ _ day __
T _ _ _ day __
S _ _ day __

b Complete the dialogues with *in, at* or *on*.

A: What time do you get up *on* Saturdays?

B: Around ten o'clock.

1 **A:** What do you do _____ the evening, after work?

   B: I play sport.

2 **A:** Do you work _____ the weekend?

   B: No, I don't. I work _____ weekdays.

3 **A:** Do you have a shower _____ the morning?

   B: No, I don't. I have a shower _____ night.

4 **A:** Are you at home _____ Friday evenings?

   B: No, I'm not. But I'm at home _____ Saturdays.

Vocabulary | verb collocations

2 Put the letters in the correct order to make collocations.

tae ifhs
eat fish

1 ustyd a gglnuaea

   _____

2 yats ta meoh

   _____

3 furs het tenterin

   _____

4 kame drsiefn

   _____

5 yas lolhe

   _____

6 lacl royu redfins

   _____

7 ypla rsopt

   _____

3 Complete the word puzzle to find the American river. Use the collocations from Exercise 2.

1 I _____ in my English class and at the gym. I have a lot of friends.

2 I _____ to my neighbour but he doesn't say anything to me.

3 I _____ in the evening and watch TV.

4 I _____ in the evening. I look at news websites or blogs.

5 I _____ on Monday evenings. I study French.

6 I _____ on Saturday mornings. I usually play football or tennis.

1	M	A	K	E	F	R	I	E	N	D	S		
	I												
2													
3													
	I												
4													
5													
	I												
6													
	P												
	I												

Grammar 1 | Present Simple: *you* (plural), *we* and *they*

4 Look at the table and complete Grace's sentences.

	GRACE AND MARLON	STEVE AND SHENA
have children	2	0
(1) play sport	no	at the weekend
(2) eat in restaurants	no	Friday and Saturday evenings
(3) like our jobs	yes	no
(4) get up early	yes	no

Grace: *We have two children*. They *don't have children*.

1 Grace: We _____ . They _____ .

2 Grace: They _____ . We _____ .

3 Grace: We _____ . They _____ .

4 Grace: We _____ . They _____ .

5 Complete the dialogue with the correct form of *do* and *like*.

WEEKEND HOUSE SWAP

Two couples swap houses for a weekend and decorate!

Presenter: So, Sasha and Liam, what *do you do*?

Sasha: We're office workers.

Presenter: And what about Colin and Nancy. What (1) _____ they _____ ?

Liam: They're teachers.

Presenter: What colours (2) _____ they _____ ?

Sasha: They (3) _____ blues and greens. But They (4) _____ _____ greys and blacks.

Presenter: What colours (5) _____ you _____ ? (6) _____ you _____ blues and greens, too?

Liam: No, we (7) _____ . We (8) _____ whites and greys. They're beautiful colours.

Presenter: OK, thanks. Happy decorating!

Grammar 2 | *Wh-* questions

6 **a** Complete the dialogues with *where, when, how, what* and *who*.

A: *Who* do you work for?
B: I work for Regent Enterprises.

1 A: _____ colours do you like?
B: I like red and green.

2 A: _____ do you live?
B: In Saint Tropez.

3 A: _____ do you start work?
B: At 8:30.

4 A: _____ do you cook paella?
B: It's easy!

5 A: _____ time do you finish work?
B: Around 5 p.m.

6 A: _____ do you live with?
B: My son and daughter.

7 A: _____ do you do?
B: I'm a doctor.

8 A: _____ do you teach?
B: I teach Spanish.

b Write questions to find the missing information.

I work for …
Who do your work for?

1 I live in …
   _____

2 I'm a …
   _____

3 I teach …
   _____

4 I start work at …
   _____

5 I live with …
   _____

Pronunciation | *do* in *Wh-* questions

7 **a** Underline the stressed words in each question.

<u>What</u> <u>sports</u> do you <u>play</u>?

1 Where do you live?
2 Who do you like?
3 When do you go to bed?
4 What do you do?

b 🔘 24 Listen, check and repeat.

Vocabulary | rooms

1 Put the letters in the correct order to make rooms and places in a house.

ritssa *stairs*

1 chitkne _____
2 larlec _____
3 tofl _____
4 habmorot _____
5 droomeb _____
6 degnra _____
7 lhla _____
8 regaga _____
9 vinlgi omro _____

Vocabulary | furniture

2 Match the words from the box with the pictures.

> armchair   basin   bath   bin   chair
> coffee table   cooker   desk   dishwasher
> fridge   lamp   mirror   sink   ~~sofa~~   table
> toilet   wardrobe   washing machine

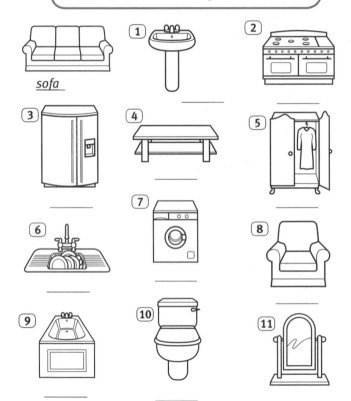

sofa

3 Match the furniture in exercise 2 to the rooms below.

Bathroom: _____ _____ _____
Bedroom: _____ _____
Kitchen: _____ _____ _____ _____
Living room: *sofa* _____ _____

Grammar | *have got*

4 a Look at the table. Complete the text for Jamie.

	Jamie	Patricia
bedrooms	1	2
garage	✗	✓
garden	✗	✗
washing machine	✓	✗
bath	✗	✓
sofa	✓	✓
car	✓	✗

'I *'ve* got a flat in Notting Hill in the UK. It (1) _____ one bedroom and a living room but it (2) _____ a garage or a garden. I (3) _____ a washing machine in the kitchen and a sofa in the living room. I (4) _____ a bath – just a shower. I (5) _____ a car – it's a small, red sports car.'

b Look at the chart. Complete the text about Patricia.

She *'s got* a house in Auckland in New Zealand. It (1) _____ two bedrooms and a garage but it (2) _____ a garden. She (3) _____ a bath in the bathroom and a sofa in the living room. She (4) _____ a washing machine and she (5) _____ a car.

Jamie

Patricia

5 Complete the dialogue with the correct words.

A: Hello. Can I help you?

B: No, thank you. I'm just looking.

A: Our televisions are on special offer today. *Have* you *got* a television?

B: Yes, I (1) _____ .

A: (2) _____ you _____ a television in your bedroom?

B: No, I (3) _____ . But I don't want a television in my bedroom. I want a washing machine for my mother.

A: (4) _____ your mother _____ a television?

B: Yes, she (5) _____ . She (6) _____ a television in her living room and another television in her bedroom. Now, how much is this washing machine?

A: It's £399. The television is only £299 ...

6 Write complete sentences with *have got*.

(you/a car?) (Yes)

A: *Have you got a car?*

B: *Yes, I have.*

1 (Ravi/✓/a new house)

   _____ .

2 (My parents/✗/a washing machine)

   _____ .

3 (your house/a garage?) (No)

   A: _____ ?

   B: _____ .

4 (that hotel/a swimming pool?) (Yes)

   A: _____ ?

   B: _____ .

5 (my hotel room/✗/bath)

   _____ .

6 (we/✓/a new baby)

   _____ .

7 (you/✓/a beautiful flat)

   _____ .

8 (my sisters/✗/any children)

   _____ .

9 (we/any milk in the fridge?) (Yes)

   A: _____ ?

   B: _____ .

Reading

7 **a** Read the texts and answer the questions with *Oscar*, *Oscar's friends*, *Rink* or *Rink's cousin*.

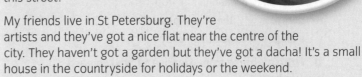

I want to live in ...

This week we talk to Oscar Sterner – actor, singer and writer, and Rink Amra – DJ and artist.

Oscar: I'm from Stockholm in Sweden but I want to live in St Petersburg in Russia. St Petersburg is Russia's cultural capital. It's only 300 years old but it has got a lot of beautiful buildings, for example The Hermitage and The Summer Palace. The main street is called Nevsky Prospect. There are a lot of shops and restaurants and all the major brands have got shops on this street.

My friends live in St Petersburg. They're artists and they've got a nice flat near the centre of the city. They haven't got a garden but they've got a dacha! It's a small house in the countryside for holidays or the weekend.

Rink: I'm a DJ from Delhi in India but I want to live in Rio de Janeiro in Brazil. Rio is Brazil's cultural capital. It's about 500 years old and it has got fantastic tourist attractions, for example Copacabana beach, Sugarloaf Mountain and, of course, carnival. There are also a lot of universities, museums and theatres.

My cousin lives in Rio. He's a singer. He's got a flat in the south of the city. He hasn't got a garden but he's got a beach close to his flat.

Who lives in Rio de Janeiro?   *Rink's cousin*

1 Who is from Stockholm?   _____

2 Who lives in St Petersburg?   _____

3 Who lives near a beach?   _____

4 Who's got a holiday house?   _____

5 Who works as a DJ?   _____

6 Who are artists?   _____

b Answer the questions.

1 What is Nevsky Prospect?

2 What is on Nevsky Prospect?

3 How old is Rio?

4 What are some of Rio's tourist attractions?

5 What does Rink's cousin do?

Vocabulary | doing housework

1 **a** Choose the correct word to complete the requests.

Can you _____ the dishwasher, please?

a iron   (b empty)   c clean

1   Can you _____ the living room, please?
    a tidy   b wash   c iron

2   Can you _____ the laundry, please?
    a wash   b clean   c do

3   Can you _____ the table, please?
    a sweep   b do   c lay

4   Can you _____ the bathroom, please?
    a lay   b wash   c clean

5   Can you _____ the floor, please?
    a tidy   b sweep   c empty

6   Can you _____ your clothes, please?
    a iron   b do   c vacuum

7   Can you _____ the dishes, please?
    a sweep   b wash   c iron

8   Can you _____ the stairs, please?
    a empty   b vacuum   c lay

b Write a phrase from exercise 1a next to each picture below.

empty the dishwasher   _____

_____   _____

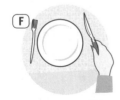

_____   _____

_____   _____

How to... | make simple requests

2 **a** Put the words in the correct order to complete the dialogues.

A: you   please?   Can   table,   the   lay
    Can you lay the table, please?

B: no   Sure,   problem.
    Sure, no problem.

1   A: dishes,   Can   wash   you   the   please?
    _____

    B: course.   Yes,   of
    _____

2   A: sweep   please?   you   Can   floor,   the
    _____

    B: sorry.   can't.   I'm   late.   I'm   I   No,
    _____

b Write new dialogues. Use the pictures and the prompts.

A: *Can you take a photo of us, please?* (take a photo of us)

B: *Sure, no problem.* (sure)

1   A: _____
    _____ ? (carry my bags)

    B: _____ . (yes)

2   A: _____
    _____ ? (answer the phone)

    B: _____ . (sorry)

Grammar | adverbs of frequency

3 **a** Complete the table with the words from the box.

> never   sometimes   usually   ~~always~~

100% ↑ 0%	*always* _____ _____ _____

b Complete the sentences with an adverb of frequency.

I watch TV in the evenings. (usually)

I usually watch TV in the evenings.

We're late for work. (always)

We're always late for work.

1   I wash the dishes. (always)

_____ .

2   She does the laundry. (sometimes)

_____ .

3   My children tidy their bedrooms. (never)

_____ .

4   The food in that restaurant is terrible. (usually)

_____ .

5   I make breakfast for my wife on Sunday.
(sometimes)

_____ .

6   He is happy on Friday afternoons. (always)

_____ .

7   I go to the gym before work. (never)

_____ .

8   Our cleaner is really fast. (usually)

_____ .

4 Correct the mistake in each sentence.

I watch never TV in the afternoon.

I never watch TV in the afternoon.

1   Maggie plays usually sport on Friday afternoon.

_____ .

2   I sometime iron her clothes.

_____ .

3   You sometimes are really sad.

_____ .

4   Never he finishes work late on Friday.

_____ .

5   Her friends always are attractive.

_____ .

6   British people are usually have a sandwich for
lunch.

_____ .

Pronunciation | /ʌ/ and /ɪ/

5 **a** 🔊 25 Listen. Which sound can you hear in
each sentence, /ʌ/ or /ɪ/?

	/ʌ/	/ɪ/
Does your mum sometimes come here?	✓	☐
1 Is my dinner in the kitchen?	☐	☐
2 I love Sundays but I hate Mondays.	☐	☐
3 Where's his business card? It's in the living room.	☐	☐

b Underline the examples of the sounds in each
sentence.

c Listen again and repeat the sentences.

Reading

6 Read the text. Complete the sentences with *Per,
Ron, Matthew* or *Felipe*.

In Japan, about 10 per cent of husbands usually do housework. In Portugal, about 20 per cent of husbands usually do the housework and in the USA, it is 35 per cent. Men, are you lazy? What housework do you do?

'My wife makes dinner but I always lay the table and empty the dishwasher. She's a good cook and I'm not! We've both got jobs and we work all week.'

Per, Sweden

'I don't do any housework but I work 60 hours a week. I come home around 8 p.m. I haven't got time for housework. My wife doesn't work. She does all the housework but I sometimes make dinner on Sunday.'

Ron, USA

'My wife usually does the housework. I sometimes tidy the living room or make dinner, but my wife usually does it. She gets up early and does it. I never get up early. I'm always tired.'

Matthew, UK

'My wife and I work about 50 hours a week. At weekends we do the housework together. For example, I usually do the laundry and she usually cleans the bathroom. We haven't got a cleaner.'

Felipe, Argentina

Matthew is always tired.

1   _____ doesn't do any housework.

2   _____ never makes dinner.

3   _____ gets up late.

4   _____ does the housework on Saturday
and Sunday.

5   _____ finishes work late.

How to... | offer food and drink

1 Complete the dialogues with the phrases from the box.

> What would you like (x2)   Yes, please
> Would you like (x2)   I'd like (x2)

1 A: Hello. Come in.
   B: Thanks.
   A: *What would you like* to drink?
   B: (1) _____ a coffee, please.
   A: (2) _____ something to eat?
   B: No, thank you.

2 A: (3) _____ a cup of tea?
   B: (4) _____ . I'd love one.
   A: Milk and sugar?
   B: Milk, no sugar, please.

3 A: (5) _____ to eat?
   B: (6) _____ a sandwich, please.
   A: Cheese? Chicken?
   B: Cheese, please.

Pronunciation | *would you*

2 **a** Underline the /dju:/ sound.

Wou<u>ld you</u> like a cup of tea?

1 Would you like something to eat?
2 What would you like to drink?
3 Would you like a cold drink?

b 26 Listen and write the sentences you hear.

What would you like to eat?

1 _____
2 _____
3 _____
4 _____

Grammar | *like + -ing; want + infinitive*

3 Complete the sentences with *want* or *like*.

Marcus and Pete *want* to play football.

1 Do you _____ eating in fast food restaurants?
2 Which restaurant do you _____ to go to?
3 They don't _____ watching TV.
4 Does she _____ playing tennis?
5 Do you _____ to go for a walk?
6 I don't _____ watching Hollywood films.
7 We _____ to go to the theatre.
8 I don't _____ working late.

4 Complete the texts with the correct form of the verbs given.

My name is Kate Watson. I'm a chef. I work for a small restaurant called The Happy Chicken. I like *being* (be) a chef and I like (1) _____ (work) with food but I don't like (2) _____ (finish) work at one o'clock in the morning. I want (3) _____ (start) work at nine and finish at five. I want (4) _____ (go) shopping with my friends at the weekend. I never see my friends – I'm always at work!

My name is Johan Holland. I'm a call centre worker. I like (5) _____ (work) with people but I don't like my job. It's not exciting. I want (6) _____ (be) a sales rep. I like (7) _____ (make) friends with people and I like (8) _____ (live) in a big city. But I don't want (9) _____ (talk) on the telephone for eight hours a day.

Vocabulary | technology

5 **a** Label the picture with six of the words from the box.

> a camcorder   a camera   a DVD player
> a flat-screen TV   a games console   a laptop
> a stereo   wireless Internet

a _____
b _____
c _____
d _____
e _____
f _____

b Complete the dialogues with a verb and a word from exercise 5a.

Do you *listen* to music much at home?
Yes, I do. I've got a *stereo* in my bedroom.

1   A: Do you _____ computer games much at home?
    B: Yes, I do. I've got a new _____ in my bedroom.

2   A: Do you _____ a lot of video?
    B: No, I don't. I haven't got a _____ .

3   A: Do you _____ TV much at home?
    B: Yes, I do. We've got a _____ in the living room.

4   A: Do you _____ the Internet much at home?
    B: Yes, I do. I've got a _____ in my bedroom and we've got _____ at home.

5   A: Do you _____ a lot of photos?
    B: No, I don't. I haven't got a _____ .

6   A: Do you _____ a lot of DVDs at home?
    B: No, I don't. We haven't got a _____ .

Listening

6 🔘 27 Cover the audioscript and listen. Complete the table.

	Jo	Lukasz
drink		*sparkling water*
food		(1)
has got	(2)	(3)
wants	(4)	(5)
likes	(6)	(7)

AUDIOSCRIPT

J: Hi. Come in, Lukasz.
L: Thanks, Jo. This is a nice house.
J: Thank you. Can I take your coat?
L: Yes. Thanks.
J: Come in. Sit down. Would you like a drink?
L: Have you got a cold drink?
J: Yes, I have. I've got apple juice, sparking water ...
L: A sparkling water, please.
J: Would you like a slice of orange cheesecake, too?
L: Mmm, yes please ... Hey, you've got a nice stereo.
J: Thanks. I really like listening to music. What about you?
L: I like listening to music, too but I haven't got a stereo. I've got a laptop. All my music is on that.
J: Oh. I haven't got a laptop. I want to get one.
L: Do you like playing computer games?
J: No, not really. I haven't got a games console. Have you?
L: Yes, I have. I really like playing computer games but my console is quite old. I want to get a new one.
J: Which console do you want to get?
L: Oh, I don't know really.
J: My brother's got a ...

Present Simple

1 Complete the sentences with the correct form of the verb in brackets.

Gary is a chef. He *starts* (start) work at five in the afternoon.

My parents *don't get up* (not get up) late at the weekend.

1 I _____ (like) British pop music.
2 My partner and I _____ (watch) TV every evening.
3 Sophie _____ (not eat) fish.
4 Sebastian _____ (not say) hello to me.
5 Alexia _____ (not like) football.
6 You _____ (finish) work late.
7 He _____ (finish) work at 5 every day.
8 Bea and Telio _____ (stay) at home on Fridays.
9 Harry's sister _____ (love) your house.
10 Grant _____ (call) his friends every evening.

2 Write questions and answers. Use the prompts.

(you/play any sport) (yes)
A: *Do you play any sport?*
B: *Yes, I do.*

1 (your sisters/like your wife) (no)
   A: _____ ?
   B: _____ .
2 (Jibril/eat a lot) (yes)
   A: _____ ?
   B: _____ .
3 (they/work from home) (yes)
   A: _____ ?
   B: _____ .
4 (Felix/love her) (no)
   A: _____ ?
   B: _____ .
5 (your friends/live in Barcelona) (yes)
   A: _____ ?
   B: _____ .
6 (Ramzi/go to bed early) (no)
   A: _____ ?
   B: _____ .
7 (we/have any food in the house?) (no)
   A: _____ ?
   B: _____ .

Wh- questions

3 Put the words in the correct order to make questions.

work? do Where you
Where do you work?

1 live? Where you do
   _____ ?
2 you What do do?
   _____ ?
3 in German? hello you How do say
   _____ ?
4 do Who for? you work
   _____ ?
5 time up? you What do get
   _____ ?
6 you What do languages study?
   _____ ?
7 When start? the does party
   _____ ?
8 Mirina does with? Who live
   _____ ?

have got

4 Complete the dialogues with the correct form of *have got*.

1 Mila: *Have* you *got* a house or a flat?
   Lilly: I (1) _____ _____ a house.
   Mila: (2) _____ it _____ a garage?
   Lilly: No, it (3) _____ . But that's OK. I (4) _____ _____ a car.
   Mila: (5) _____ you _____ a garden?
   Lilly: No, I (6) _____ but my friends (7) _____ _____ a garden and I sometimes go there. They (8) _____ _____ a swimming pool in their garden, too.
   Mila: Wow! (9) _____ they _____ a tennis court, too?
   Lilly: Yes, they (10) _____ .

2 Archie: (11) _____ your brother _____ a games console?
   Sadiq: Yes, he (12) _____ .
   Archie: What console (13) _____ he _____?
   Sadiq: He (14) _____ _____ an Xbox 360.
   Archie: I (15) _____ _____ a 360, too.
   Sadiq: (16) _____ you _____ *Metal Wars*?
   Archie: No, I (17) _____ . Is it good?
   Sadiq: It's amazing.

Adverbs of frequency

5 Complete the sentences with the adverbs of frequency in brackets.

I go to bed early. (never)

I never go to bed early.

1   I'm late. (usually)

_____ .

2   Do you work from home? (sometimes)

_____ ?

3   Are they happy? (always)

_____ ?

4   I have a coffee in the morning. (usually)

_____ .

5   Do you make dinner? (sometimes)

_____ ?

6   She is late. (never)

_____ .

7   They clean the bathroom. (never)

_____ .

8   We get up before 9 o'clock at the weekend. (always)

_____ .

like + ing; want + infinitive

6 Write full sentences. Use the prompts.

(Adriana/like/sing)

Adriana likes singing.

(Peter/want/go out later)

Peter wants to go out later.

1   (My sister/not like/do the laundry)

_____ .

2   (Sol and Kay/not want/go swimming)

_____ .

3   (Alan/like/play football)

_____ .

4   (teachers/not like/finish work late)

_____ .

5   (I/not want/make dinner tonight)

_____ .

6   (Tom/want/meet Penelope)

_____ .

7   (you/like/play sport?)

_____ .

8   (Ewa and Adam/like/watch TV)

_____ .

Vocabulary

7 Complete the dialogues with the phrases from the box.

> empty the dishwasher   ~~wash the dishes~~
> go to bed   stay at home   finish work
> say hello   play sport   make dinner
> do the laundry

A: There aren't any clean dishes.

B: Why don't you *wash the dishes*, then?

1   A: I don't want to go out tonight.

   B: Why don't you _____ , then?

2   A: I'm a bit overweight.

   B: Why don't you _____ , then?

3   A: I'm always tired.

   B: Why don't you _____ early, then?

4   A: I always come home late.

   B: Why don't you _____ early, then?

5   A: All the plates and cups are in the dishwasher.

   B: Why don't you _____ , then?

6   A: I'm hungry.

   B: Why don't you _____ , then?

7   A: I think he's an old friend from school.

   B: Why don't you _____ to him, then?

8   A: I haven't got any clean clothes.

   B: Why don't you _____ , then?

8 Choose the odd one out.

	a	b
	a basin	b overweight
	c sofa	d wardrobe
1	a camera	b laptop
	c games console	d cellar
2	a attractive	b armchair
	c slim	d ugly
3	a quarter to five	b seventy five
	c twenty past two	d ten o'clock
4	a Sunday	b Wednesday
	c Friday	d bathroom
5	a mirror	b bedroom
	c garage	d loft
6	a camcorder	b stereo
	c bin	d wireless internet
7	a sink	b old
	c short	d tall
8	a hall	b living room
	c flat-screen TV	d kitchen
9	a half past one	b quarter to nine
	c twelve years old	d twenty to three
10	a Thursday	b Tuesday
	c birthday	d Monday

7 Leisure

Vocabulary | leisure activities

1 **a** Match the photos with the leisure activities from the box.

> aerobics   chess   cycling   exercise
> a gallery   puzzles   ~~tennis~~   a walk

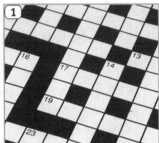

tennis

b Complete the table with the words from Exercise 1a.

play	*chess* _____
do	_____ _____ _____
go for	_____
go to	_____
go + *-ing*	_____

Vocabulary | verbs of like and dislike

2 **a** Choose the correct verb.

☺☺

I *like*/*don't mind*/*hate* chess.

1 ☺
My parents *don't like*/*don't mind*/*love* football.

2 ☺☺☺
She *quite likes*/*loves*/*doesn't mind* my music.

3 ☹☹
My brother *hates*/*likes*/*doesn't like* tennis.

4 ☹☹☹
I *hate*/*love*/*quite like* going to galleries.

5 ☺
My cousin *doesn't mind*/*loves*/*quite likes* doing puzzles.

b Look at the table. Write sentences about twins Bella and Olive.

	Bella	Olive
do exercise	☺☺☺	☹☹
1 go to galleries	☹☹☹	☺
2 Twitter	☺	☹☹
3 stay at home on a Saturday night	☺☺	☹☹☹
4 do puzzles	☺	☺☺☺
5 sushi	☹☹	☺

Bella: *'I love doing exercise but Olive doesn't like it.'*

1 Olive: '_____.'
2 Bella: '_____.'
3 Olive: '_____.'
4 Bella: '_____.'
5 Olive: '_____.'

How to... | make suggestions

3 **a** Complete the dialogues with the words in the box.

> Let's   nice   ~~Shall~~   sure   Why   Yes

1 A: _Shall_ we go for a walk in the park?
   B: I'm not _____ . I'm quite tired.
2 A: _____ go cycling. It's nice weather.
   B: _____ , OK.
3 A: _____ don't we play chess?
   B: OK. That sounds _____ .

b Write three new dialogues. Use the prompts.

A: (Shall/cycling?)   _Shall we go cycling?_
B: (OK/nice)   _OK. That sounds nice._
1 A: (Let's/a puzzle) _____ .
   B: (not sure/busy) _____ .
2 A: (why/tennis)   _____ ?
   B: (OK/nice)   _____ .
3 A: (shall/walk)   _____ ?
   B: (OK)   _____ .

Pronunciation | /aɪ/ and /eɪ/

4 **a** 🔘 28 Listen. Write the words you hear.

like

1 _____
2 _____
3 _____
4 _____
5 _____

b Match /aɪ/ or /eɪ/ to each word in exercise 4a.

/aɪ/

1 _____
2 _____
3 _____
4 _____
5 _____

c Listen again and repeat the words.

5 **a** Say the sentences. Then underline the /aɪ/ and /eɪ/ sounds in each sentence.

Do you like cycling?

1 Do you hate playing tennis?
2 I don't mind getting up at eight.

b 🔘 29 Listen, check and repeat.

Grammar | object pronouns

6 **a** Complete the sentences. Write the object pronoun form of the word in **bold**.

I like Bob but he doesn't like _me_.
1 **We** don't like the Johnsons but they quite like
   _____ .
2 **She** loves John and John loves _____ .
3 **He**'s always angry but I quite like _____ .
4 **You** are attractive but I don't love _____ .
5 Where are **they**? I really like _____ .

b Complete the dialogue with object pronouns.

Man: Here, this ice cream is for _you_. It's your favourite, chocolate.
Woman: Thanks.
Man: And this one is for (1) _____ . It's my favourite, strawberry.
Woman: Who is the drink for; (2) _____ or me?
Man: It's for you and me. It's for both of (3) _____ .
Woman: The film starts in five minutes. It's a Johnny Depp film.
Man: Johnny Depp? I like (4) _____ . Do you like the *Pirates of the Caribbean* films?
Woman: Yes, I love (5) _____ . Do you know *Chocolat*?
Man: Yes, I really like (6) _____ . It's a great film.
Woman: Johnny Depp's wife is French. Her name's Vanessa Paradis. She's a singer.
Man: Vanessa Paradis. I don't know (7) _____ .
Woman: She's really beautiful. The film's starting.
Person: Ssh!
Woman: Sorry!

Vocabulary | abilities

1   **a**   Match the verbs in A to the nouns in B.

	A		B
1	use a	a	a car
2	dance	b	dinner
3	play	c	computer
4	write	d	French
5	cook	e	the tango
6	drive	f	the piano
7	sing	g	a song
8	talk to	h	computer programmes
9	speak	i	animals

b   Complete the sentences with a phrase from Exercise 1a in the correct form.

My brother _writes computer programmes_ in his free time.

I want to learn to _____ _____ .

I _____ _____ every day.

I don't know how to _____ .

I don't want to _____ _____ tonight.

Can people _____ _____ ?

Bonjour!

Do you want to learn to _____ ?

Do you want to _____ _____ with me?

Grammar | can/can't

2   Write sentences with *can* and *can't*. Use the prompts.

(I/sing ✓/play the piano ✗)

I can sing but I can't play the piano.

1   (Jim and Jane/cook ✓/drive ✗)

_____ .

2   (Ibrahim/swim ✓/use a computer ✗)

_____ .

3   (We/play chess ✗/play the piano ✓)

_____ .

4   (Jing/use a computer ✓/write computer programmes ✗)

_____ .

5   (We/drive ✗/dance ✓)

_____ .

3   Complete the dialogue with the phrases from the box.

> can   Can he   ~~can you~~   Can you   he can
> he can't   I can   I can't   They can

A: So, Mrs Redwood, _can you_ speak Italian?

B: Yes, (1) _____ . My mother and father are from Switzerland. (2) _____ speak Italian, English, French and German.

A: Great. (3) _____ speak French and German too?

B: I (4) _____ speak German but (5) _____ speak French.

A: OK. The manager, Mr Harris, is from France so (6) _____ speak French. But he can speak Italian, too.

B: Really? That's great! (8) _____ speak German?

A: No, (7) _____ .

4 a Look at the table. Complete Erica's sentences.

Me (Erica)	Jo (my sister)	Eddie (my brother)	My parents

play the piano

Erica: I can *play the piano but my sister, Jo, can't.*

1 drive

   Erica: My brother, Eddie, _____
   _____ .

2 swim

   Erica: My brother, Eddie, _____
   _____ .

3 sing

   Erica: My sister, Jo, _____
   _____ .

b Look at the table in exercise 4a and write questions and answers. Use the prompts.

(your brother/swim?)

A: *Can your brother, Eddie, swim?*

B: *Yes, he can.*

1 (your parents/use a computer?)

   A: _____ ?

   B: _____ .

2 (your sister/play the piano?)

   A: _____ ?

   B: _____ .

3 (you/dance?)

   A: _____ ?

   B: _____ .

Pronunciation | *can* and *can't*

5 a 🔵 30 Listen. Write the sentences you hear.

Can you speak English?

1 _____

2 _____

3 _____

4 _____

5 _____

b Listen again and say the sentences.

Reading

6 Read the article and answer the questions.

Men and women:
are they the same or are they different?

Some people think that men and women are very different. For example, some people think that men can read maps but women can't. Felix Alden is a writer. His book *Men and Women* is very popular. He thinks that women can listen to people's problems, for example, but men can't. And he thinks that men can read maps but women can't.

Other people think that men and women are very similar. Janet Prokopowicz is a writer, too. Her book *The Male Mind and the Female Mind* is also very popular. She thinks that men and women aren't very different. 'Men and women learn different abilities at home and at school,' Prokopowicz says, 'but men and women are really the same.'

What do you think?

What is Felix Alden's job?

He's a writer.

1 What is the name of his book?

   _____

2 Does he think that men and women are the same or different?

   _____

3 What is Janet Prokopowicz's job?

   _____

4 What is the name of her book?

   _____

5 Does she think that men and women are the same or different?

   _____

Vocabulary | months

1 a Complete the months. Then put them in the correct order.

J u l y ☐
__ c t __ b __ r ☐
J __ n __ __ r y ☐ 1
D __ c __ m b __ r ☐
__ __ g __ s t ☐
M __ y ☐
__ p r __ l ☐
F __ b r __ __ r __ ☐
N __ v __ m b __ r ☐
J __ n __ ☐
S __ p t __ m b __ r ☐
M __ r c h ☐

b Cover the months in Exercise 1a. What month is the birthday of each celebrity below?

Maria Sharapova (19/04/1987)
April

1 Giorgio Armani (11/07/1934)
_____

2 Michelle Obama (17/01/1964)
_____

3 Roger Federer (08/08/1981)
_____

4 Rihanna (20/02/1988)
_____

5 Bruce Springsteen (23/09/1949)
_____

6 Woody Allen (1/12/1935)
_____

7 Bono (10/05/1960)
_____

8 Angelina Jolie (04/06/1975)
_____

9 Sting (02/10/1951)
_____

10 Javier Bardem (01/03/1969)
_____

11 Calvin Klein (10/11/1942)
_____

Vocabulary | ordinal numbers

2 Complete the crossword with the written form of the numbers.

Across	Down
2 4th	1 5th
5 30th	3 12th
7 11th	4 15th
10 19th	6 20th
11 8th	8 1st
12 3rd	9 2nd

How to... | write and say dates

3 Complete the table with the spoken or written forms of the dates.

Spoken	Written
the twenty-first of January	*21st January*
the eleventh of March	*11th March*
the first of May	(1) _____
(2) _____	12th December
the twentieth of June	(3) _____
the sixteenth of November	(4) _____
(5) _____	2nd September
(6) _____	3rd February
the twelfth of October	(7) _____
(8) _____	30th April
the ninth of July	(9) _____

Grammar | *in, at, on*

4 Choose the correct word: *in, at* or *on*.

Is your birthday (in) / *at* / *on* June?

1 My party is *in* / *at* / *on* 13th July.
2 Let's go on holiday *in* / *at* / *on* the beginning of August.
3 I've got two tickets for the theatre *in* / *at* / *on* 14th May.
4 Shall we go cycling *in* / *at* / *on* Sunday?
5 The football match starts *in* / *at* / *on* 3 o'clock.
6 I don't like going on holiday *in* / *at* / *on* August.
7 My daughter starts school *in* / *at* / *on* the end of this month.
8 Are you free *in* / *at* / *on* Wednesday evening?
9 Is there a show *in* / *at* / *on* the afternoon?

5 Write complete questions. Use the prompts.

be/your birthday/January?

Is your birthday in January?

match/finish/5 o'clock?

Does the match finish at 5 o'clock?

1 your new job/start/beginning of April?

_____
_____ ?

2 be/the show sold out/end of June?

_____
_____ ?

3 you/want/go out/Friday evening?

_____
_____ ?

4 shall/go to the theatre/3rd March?

_____
_____ ?

5 be/her birthday/June?

_____
_____ ?

6 the film/start/half past seven?

_____
_____ ?

Listening

6 a 🔊 31 Listen. Match the dialogues (1–3) with the pictures (A–C).

dialogue ___   dialogue ___

dialogue ___

b Listen again and complete the table.

	what?	when?	why not?
1	*go to the theatre*		
2			
3			

AUDIOSCRIPT

1

M: Hey, Adam, it's Mary.
A: Hi, Mary. How are you?
M: Fine, thanks. Adam, I've got two tickets for the theatre on 19th April. Do you want to come with me?
A: What day is that?
M: It's a Saturday.
A: OK, that sounds nice. Oh, no, wait a minute. I can't. That's my sister's birthday.
M: Oh, that's a shame. Never mind.
A: I'm really sorry.
M: Don't worry. Another time. How are things with you?

2

B: Helen?
H: Yes?
B: Let's go on holiday in July.
H: Where to?
B: Scotland. There's a really cheap deal on the Internet.
H: When in July?
B: From 8th to 15th.
H: It's your brother's birthday party on 10th July.
B: Oh yes! That's a shame. Never mind.

3

R: Are you OK, Mrs Cranfield?
C: Yes, thank you, Rebecca.
R: Do you want anything?
C: No, thank you, dear.
R: A cup of tea?
C: No, thank you. Oh, just one thing. When is the trip to the beach? Is it on 28th or 29th August?
R: It's on 29th August. That's two weeks from now.
C: Oh, lovely. Thank you.

Vocabulary | saying years

1 Complete the table.

Written	Spoken
1989	*nineteen eighty-nine*
1 2004	_____
2 1803	_____
3 1909	_____
4 1970	_____
5 2012	_____
6 1881	_____
7 1999	_____
8 2015	_____

2 **a** 🔘 32 Cover the audioscript and listen. Write the dates next to each picture.

Date: *1st July 1941*
Other information:
10 seconds $9

1

Date: _____
Other information:
_____
_____

2

Date: _____
Other information:
_____
_____

3

Date: _____
Other information:
_____
_____

b Listen again. Write other information next to the pictures.

AUDIOSCRIPT

The first TV advert was on 1st July 1941. It was ten seconds long and the cost was just nine dollars.

1 The first newspaper crossword was on 21st December 1913. It was called a 'Word-cross'.

2 The first mobile phone call was on 3rd April 1973. It was in New York.

3 The first tourist in space was on 28th April 2001. His name was Dennis Tito.

Vocabulary | jobs

3 **a** Complete the words to make jobs.

sp<u>o</u>rts st<u>a</u>r

1 p__l__t__c__ __n
2 sc__ __nt__st
3 s__ng__r
4 wr__t__r
5 m__s__c__ __n
6 b__s__n__ss p__rs__n
7 __ct__r
8 __rt__st
9 d__nc__r
10 l__ __d__r

b Look at the photos 1–9. Complete the word puzzle to find the hidden job.

Grammar | Past Simple of *to be*: positive

4 Complete the texts with *was* and *were*.

1 Frida Kahlo *was* a Mexican painter. She (1) _____ born in Mexico City in 1907. Her parents (2) _____ Guillermo and Matilde. Frida (3) _____ the third of four daughters. She (4) _____ a medical student in the early 1920s and then a painter: 'I (5) _____ born a painter,' Frida said. A lot of her 200 paintings (6) _____ self-portraits. Frida (7) _____ 47 when she died. Now she is an international icon.

2 The Beatles (8) _____ John, Paul, George and Ringo. They (9) _____ from Liverpool. Their first name (10) _____ *The Quarrymen*. In 1961 they (11) _____ popular in Liverpool and Hamburg. Their first hit, in 1962, (12) _____ *Love Me Do*. Their next song, *Please Please Me*, (13) _____ number one in early 1963. *Revolver* and *Let It Be* (14) _____ popular Beatles albums.

5 Rewrite these sentences in the Past Simple with *was* or *were*.

Jeff and I are late for the party.
Jeff and I were late for the party.

1 My son and daughter are at home.

_____

2 I'm a singer.

_____

3 You're my best friend.

_____

4 They're at school.

_____

5 She's a teacher in Australia.

_____

Pronunciation | /ɜ:/

6 a 🔘 33 Choose the two words with the /ɜ:/ sound.

(a) were   b see   c here   (d) first

1 a three   b thirty   c third   d four
2 a person   b sure   c birthday   d horse
3 a late   b early   c friend   d word

b Listen and check.

Reading

7 a Read the webpage. Match the headings (a–d) with the gaps (1–4).

a The first World Cup
b The first Internet celebrity
c The first billionaire
d The first president of the USA

Four Famous Firsts

(1) ____
Most people think that George Washington was first. But it was Samuel Huntington in 1779. George Washington was the first president under the new constitution in 1789.

(2) ____
A billion dollars is $1,000,000,000 (one thousand million). Today's billionaires are Bill Gates, Carlos Slim and a few others. But the first billionaire was John D. Rockerfeller in 1916. His company, Standard Oil, was very big in the late 19th and early 20th centuries.

John D. Rockerfeller

(3) ____
It was in Uruguay in 1930. There were thirteen countries in the competition. Argentina and Uruguay were the two teams in the final and Uruguay were the winners, 4–2.

(4) ____
The first one was probably a Turkish man called Mahir Cagri. His website was very simple. The first words were 'Welcome to my home page. I kiss you!' Soon there were 12 million visitors to his website and he was called the 'I Kiss You guy'.

b Read the webpage again. Are the sentences true (T) or false (F)?

George Washington was the first president of the USA. *F*

1 Samuel Huntington was the President of the USA in 1779. ___
2 Bill Gates was the first billionaire. ___
3 Standard Oil was John D. Rockerfeller's company. ___
4 The first World Cup was in Argentina. ___
5 The first World Cup winner was Uruguay. ___
6 The first Internet celebrity was from Turkey. ___
7 There were a lot of visitors to Mahir's website. ___

Vocabulary | past time expressions

1 **a** Read the text. Put the pictures in time order.

My dad is a business person. He works for Trans-Global Software. He travels abroad a lot. For example, last week he was in Moscow and two weeks ago, at the start of June, he was in New York. Three days ago he was in Athens, yesterday he was in London and in May he was in Paris. He never stops!

b Complete the sentences with *yesterday, ago, last* or *in*.

I was ill __last__ week.

1   Where were you _____ morning?
2   My last holiday was _____ 2010.
3   There was someone at my door at twelve o'clock _____ night.
4   She was my teacher ten years _____ .
5   Was he at school _____ Monday?
6   It was very cold _____ week.
7   Sandy's party was three days _____ .
8   Where was your friend, Billy, _____ evening?
9   Ursula was a student _____ year. Now she's a teacher.
10 Your shoes were cool _____ 1985.

Grammar | Past Simple of *to be*: negatives and questions

2 **a** Read the profile and write complete sentences. Use the prompts.

Cate/born/the UK

Cate wasn't born in the UK. She was born in Australia.

1   Her parents/born/the UK
    _____

2   She/a good singer/at school
    _____

3   She/an English student/at university
    _____

4   Her first big film/*Elizabeth I*
    _____

5   Roman/born/2003
    _____

Cate Blanchett

PROFILE

Name:	Catherine Elise Blanchett
Born:	14th May, 1969, in Melbourne, Australia
Father:	Robert Blanchett, from the USA
Mother:	June Blanchett, from Australia
Childhood:	good actor at school
University:	Melbourn University (Economics)
First big film:	*Oscar and Lucinda*
Children:	Dashiell (born 2001), Roman (born 2004), Ignatius (born 2008)

b Write questions and answers. Use the prompts from exercise 2a.

Was Cate born in the UK?

No, she wasn't.

1 _____ ?
_____ .

2 _____ ?
_____ .

3 _____ ?
_____ .

4 _____ ?
_____ .

5 _____ ?
_____ .

3 Complete the dialogue with *was, wasn't, were* or *weren't*.

Interviewer: So, Melissa, congratulations on your Grammy award.

Melissa: Thank you! I'm so excited.

Interviewer: When you *were* a child, (1) _____ you a good singer?

Melissa: No, I (2) _____ . I (3) _____ a very bad singer. But my two music teachers at high school (4) _____ great.

Interviewer: Who (5) _____ your music teachers?

Melissa: Their names (6) _____ Mrs Felton and Mr Herbert. They (7) _____ really good!

Interviewer: Who (8) _____ your favourite singers when you were a teenager?

Melissa: My favourite female singer (9) _____ Aretha Franklin and my favourite male singer was Louis Armstrong.

Interviewer: (10) _____ your parents singers?

Melissa: No, they (11) _____ . My mother (12) _____ a scientist and my father (13) _____ a househusband.

4 Correct the mistakes.

Was you a good singer when you were young?

Were you a good singer when you were young?

1 Richard and Alex isn't at work yesterday.
_____

2 Were your father a politician?
_____

3 Were Ronald Reagan a film star?
_____

4 My father not a singer but he was a musician.
_____

5 Was you at home last night?
_____

6 When were your last holiday?
_____

7 Who your best friend was at school?
_____

8 What were Marlon Brando's last film?
_____

How to... | take part in a game

5 **a** Choose the correct phrase.

a (Is it my go?)
b Is my go?
c Is it my come?

1 a Good done!
b Well done!
c Best done!

2 a Don't mind!
b Not mind!
c Never mind!

3 a Oh no! No again!
b Oh no! Not again!
c Oh no! Again not!

4 a Yes! I win!
b Yes! I am win!
c Yes! I winner!

b Complete the dialogue with the words from the box.

| again done ~~go~~ mind Roll win |

A: Is it my *go*?
B: Yes, it's your go. (1) _____ the dice.
A: Oh no! Not (2) _____ !
B: Bad luck! Never (3) _____ .
A: It's your go, now.
B: Six! Yes! I (4) _____ .
A: Well (5) _____ ! That was great.

holiday

① _____

② _____

③ _____

④ _____

How to... | ask about a past experience

1 **a** Match the words from the box with the pictures (1–4).

> date   flight   holiday   ~~trip~~   weekend

b Complete the dialogues with a word from exercise 1a and a word from the box.

> awful   attractive   fantastic   ~~good~~   fine

A: How was your *trip* to Paris?
B: It was OK. The journey was fine but the hotel wasn't very *good*.

1   A: How was your _____ ?
    B: It was _____ . It was really long and the food was terrible.

2   A: How was your _____ ?
    B: It was great. She was very nice and really _____ .

3   A: How was your _____ ?
    B: _____ , thanks. I was in town on Saturday and I was at home on Sunday.

4   A: How was your _____ ?
    B: It was _____ ! The hotel was great and the food was very nice!

Pronunciation | /aʊ/

2 **a** Choose the words with the /aʊ/ sound.
Wow! That's a big brown cow!

1   I want to go to town now to buy some flowers.
2   How tall is that mountain? About two thousand metres?
3   Mouse is a noun but how do you pronounce it?

b ⬤ 34 Listen, check and repeat.

Vocabulary | more adjectives

3 **a** Put the letters in the correct order to make adjectives.

latl   *tall*   3   ahyve   _____
1   raf   _____   4   olng   _____
2   eped   _____   5   iwed   _____

b Circle the correct adjective.

A: He's over two metres.
B: That's really *deep/far/long/tall*.

1   A: The shop is twenty kilometres from here.
    B: That's really *far/long/tall/wide*.

2   A: Her new baby is six kilogrammes!
    B: That's really *deep/heavy/long/tall*.

3   A: It's over 100 metres to the bottom of this lake.
    B: That's really *far/long/deep/wide*.

4   A: The flight is twelve hours.
    B: That's really *far/heavy/deep/long*.

5   A: The table is one metre by two metres.
    B: That's not very *deep/far/wide/tall*.

Grammar | How + adjectives

4 **a** Put the words in the correct order to make quiz questions.

the Taj Mahal   old   How   is   India?   in

How old is the Taj Mahal in India?

a It's about 360 years old.

b It's about 560 years old.

c It's about 760 years old.

① from   is   New York   How   London?   far

_____

a It's about 1500 kilometres.

b It's about 3500 kilometres.

c It's about 5500 kilometres.

② the Pacific Ocean?   is   How   in   deep the Mariana Trench

_____

a It's about 11 kilometres deep.

b It's about 51 kilometres deep.

c It's about 111 kilometres deep.

③ Napoleon?   tall   was   How

_____

a He was about 1 metre 30 centimetres tall.

b He was about 1 metre 50 centimetres tall.

c He was about 1 metre 70 centimetres tall.

④ Route 66   in   long   the USA?   is   How

_____

a About 400 kilometres.

b About 4000 kilometres.

c About 14000 kilometres.

⑤ the Grand Canyon?   How   wide   is

_____

a In some places it's thirty kilometres wide.

b In some places it's sixty kilometres wide.

c In some places it's ninety kilometres wide.

⑥ Japan?   How   in   is   Mount Fuji   tall

_____

a About 1770 metres tall.

b About 3770 metres tall.

c About 5770 metres tall.

⑦ Ayres Rock   How   Australia?   long   in   is

_____

a About 1 kilometre long, 500 metres wide and 50 metres tall.

b About 2 kilometres long, 1 kilometres wide and 200 metres tall.

c About 3.5 kilometres long, 2 kilometres wide and 350 metres tall.

b Choose the correct answers. Then check below.

0a, 1c, 2a, 3c, 4b, 5a, 6b, 7c

Listening

5 **a** 🔘 35 Cover the audioscript and listen. Answer the questions.

What does Marianne want?

A job in The Coffee Palace.

1 Where is The Coffee Palace?

_____

2 What was Marianne's last job?

_____

3 What is Favourite Fashions?

_____

4 How long was Marianne there?

_____

5 How many cafés has Carl got?

_____

6 How old is the business?

b Listen again. Complete the audioscript.

AUDIOSCRIPT

A: Take a seat. I'm Carl Sarandon.

B: I'm Marianne. Nice to meet you.

A: Nice to meet you, too. *Would* you like a coffee?

B: No, thank you.

A: How was your journey here?

B: It was (1) _____ , thank you.

A: So, you want a job in The Coffee Palace.

B: Yes, that's right.

A: What (2) _____ your last job?

B: I was a sales assistant in a clothes shop.

A: Was that here in Chicago?

B: No, it (3) _____ . It was in San Diego. I'm from California.

A: I see. What was the name of the shop?

B: Favourite Fashions.

A: Was (4) _____ your first job?

B: Yes, it was.

A: How long were you with Favourite Fashions?

B: About two years.

A: Can you make good coffee?

B: I can make great coffee.

A: Good! Do you have any (5) _____ for me?

B: Yes, is this your business?

A: Yes, it is. I've got two other cafés.

B: How (6) _____ is the business?

A: It's about three years old.

B: OK. Thank you.

A: Now, we start work here at seven in the morning ...

Object pronouns

1 Complete the sentences with the words in the box.

> her ~~him~~ it me them us you

He's my best friend. I really like *him*.

1 You're my brother and I love _____ .
2 They're really great. We like _____ a lot.
3 It's an ugly city. I don't like _____ .
4 I'm so happy. He loves _____ and I love him.
5 She's not my friend. I hate _____ .
6 We like Rex and Bobby and they like _____ .
7 Federico is OK. I don't mind _____ .

can/can't

2 Put the words in the correct order to make sentences and questions.

daughter   Can   drive?   your

Can your daughter drive?

1 can't   Jovita   aerobics.   do
_____ .

2 Spanish.   speak   They   can
_____ .

3 you   a   use   Can   computer?
_____ ?

4 dance.   can   sing   and   brothers   Your
_____ .

5 cook.   husband   My   can't
_____ .

6 son   write   programmes?   Can   computer   your
_____ ?

7 animals.   People   talk   can't   to
_____ .

8 parents   play   Can   piano?   your   the
_____ ?

3 Write sentences and questions. Use the prompts.

do aerobics (✓)/dance (✗)/play football (?)

Mr Jones can do aerobics but he can't dance.
Can he play football?

1 do puzzles (✓)/play the piano (✗)/play chess (?)
Your children _____ .
_____ ?

2 speak French (✓)/cook French food (✗)/read French books (?)
You _____ .
_____ ?

3 use a computer (✓)/write computer programmes (✗)/play computer games (?)
Mimi _____ .
_____ ?

in, at, on

4 Complete the dialogues. Add *in, at* or *on* to each sentence.

A: Are you free January?
A: *Are you free in January?*
B: No, I'm not, but I'm free the beginning of February.
B: *No, I'm not, but I'm free at the beginning of February.*

1 A: Is the party Friday?
  A: _____
  B: No, it isn't. It's Saturday.
  B: _____

2 A: Does Ramadan start the beginning of August this year?
  A: _____
  B: No, it doesn't. It starts the end of July.
  B: _____

3 A: She was born 2005.
  A: _____
  B: No she wasn't. She was born the end of 2004.
  B: _____

4 A: Do you start your new job 21st March?
  A: _____
  B: No, I don't. I start it 28th March.
  B: _____

5 A: The match starts 3:30.
  A: _____
  B: No, it doesn't. It starts 3p.m.
  B: _____

Past Simple of *be*

5 Complete the dialogue with the correct past form of *be*.

A: ... and now we've got my favourite actor in the studio. Please welcome Roxanna Milea.
B: Thank you.
A: So, Roxanne, where *were* you born?
B: I (1) _____ born in Timisoara in Romania.
A: You're a famous actor now but (2) _____ you an actor when you (3) _____ young?
B: Yes, I (4) _____ . My first job as an actor (5) _____ when I (6) _____ eight years old.
A: Eight years old? (7) _____ it a film?
B: No, it (8) _____ . It (9) _____ a TV show.
A: (10) _____ your parents actors?
B: No, they (11) _____ . My mother (12) _____ a university lecturer and my father (13) _____ a factory worker. But my brothers (14) _____ actors, like me ...

6 Write questions with the correct past form of be. Use the prompts.

Where/he born?

Where was he born?

you/a good singer?

Were you a good singer?

1 What/their names?

_____?

2 he/a teacher?

_____?

3 Where/she yesterday?

_____?

4 When/your birthday?

_____?

5 How/your holiday?

_____?

6 he/your best friend?

_____?

7 they/good friends?

_____?

Questions with *How*

7 Put the words in the correct order to make questions.

that is building? tall How

How tall is that building?

flight? How your was

How was your flight?

1 long flight? was How your

_____?

2 swimming How pool? is the deep

_____?

3 the was party? How

_____?

4 her far How house? is

_____?

5 date? your How was

_____?

6 is bag? heavy your How

_____?

7 wide her is How garden?

_____?

Vocabulary

8 Choose the correct verb.

How often do you ____ to a gallery?

a go b play c do

1 How often do you ____ tennis?

a go b play c do

2 How often do you ____ the piano?

a go b play c do

3 How often do you ____ aerobics?

a go b play c do

4 How often do you ____ a computer?

a write b use c do

5 How often do you ____ exercise?

a go b play c do

6 How often do you ____ for a walk?

a go b use c do

7 How often do you ____ puzzles?

a go b play c do

8 How often do you ____ chess?

a go b play c do

9 Complete the dialogues. Write the date as you say it.

A: What's your date of birth?

B: *It's the fourteenth of August, nineteen eighty-nine.* (14/08/1989)

A: When's your birthday?

B: *It's the ninth of November.* (9/11)

1 A: What's your date of birth?

B: _____ . (11/3/1995)

2 A: What date is New Year's Eve?

B: _____ . (31/12)

3 A: What date is New Year's Day?

B: _____ . (1/1)

4 A: What's the date today?

B: _____ . (20/9)

5 A: When is her birthday?

B: _____ . (10/6)

6 A: What's his date of birth?

B: _____ . (8/4/2009)

10 Write the name of the job.

She dances.

She's a dancer.

1 He sings.

_____ .

2 They write.

_____ .

3 She works in business.

_____ .

4 He makes music.

_____ .

5 They work in science.

_____ .

6 She acts.

_____ .

7 They make art.

_____ .

8 They play sport for a job.

_____ .

9 She is in politics.

_____ .

Vocabulary | money verbs

1 Choose the correct word to complete each dialogue.

A: Can you _____ me some money? I just need €10.

B: I'm sorry. I haven't got any money at the moment.

a borrow   (b) lend   c pay

1 A: Can I _____ by credit card?

B: No, I'm sorry. We don't take credit cards.

a pay   b spend   c buy

2 A: How much do you _____ in your new job?

B: About €150 a day.

a win   b earn   c pay

3 A: Dad, can I _____ some money?

B: No! I lend you money every week.

a win   b lend   c borrow

4 A: Where do you _____ your clothes?

B: From a shop on Paul Remy Street.

a buy   b pay   c spend

5 A: How much do you _____ on eating in restaurants every month?

B: About €40.

a spend   b buy   c pay

6 A: Why don't you _____ some money every month?

B: No. I like spending it.

a borrow   b buy   c save

7 A: I don't use this mobile phone any more.

B: Why don't you _____ it online?

a save   b sell   c invest

8 A: Look! This is my new car.

B: Wow! It's really nice. Did you _____ some money?

a lend   b buy   c win

9 A: Do you want to _____ some money in my new business?

B: What sort of business is it?

a invest   b lend   c pay

Vocabulary | teenagers and money

2 a Match 1–8 with a–h to make common teenage jobs.

1	wash	a	tidy at home
2	stack	b	your brother with his homework
3	work	c	newspapers
4	clean and	d	after your neighbours' children
5	help	e	nights in a factory
6	look	f	time
7	deliver	g	cars
8	work part-	h	shelves

b Complete the advice for teenagers. Use the jobs from Exercise 2a.

A: I sleep in the day and I'm awake at night.

B: Why don't you *work nights in a factory*?

1 A: I like maths and science but my brother doesn't.

B: Why don't you _____ ?

2 A: I like working with other people, for example in a shop.

B: Why don't you _____ ?

3 A: I like children.

B: Why don't you _____ ?

4 A: I like being at home.

B: Why don't you _____ ?

5 A: I like getting up early and going out for a walk.

B: Why don't you _____ ?

6 A: I don't want to work long hours.

B: Why don't you _____ ?

7 A: I like working outside.

B: Why don't you _____ ?

Grammar | Past Simple: regular verbs: positive

3 Rewrite the sentences in the Past Simple.

I surf the Internet for three hours every day.

I surfed the Internet for three hours last night.

1 My sister helps me with my homework.

_____ yesterday.

2 He invests all his money in shares.

_____ .

3 I borrow money from my parents.

_____ last week.

4 My friends stack shelves in a supermarket.

_____ when they were teenagers.

5 We work nights in a factory.

_____ last year.

6 I wash my father's car.

_____ last Saturday.

7 That boy delivers our newspapers.

_____ this morning.

8 He saves all his money. He hates spending it.

_____ .

4 Complete the email with the Past Simple form of the verbs from the box.

> cook clean help live look move play start
> want ~~work~~

Hello Lydia,

How are you? I'm in Madrid. This is my first time here in 15 years! It's all very different now.

When I was here last time I was a teenager. I *worked* as an au pair and (1) _____ with a Spanish family. They were very nice but it was hard work. I (2) _____ work at 6:30a.m. every morning! In the day, I (3) _____ the house and practised my Spanish. In the evening, I (4) _____ after the children and (5) _____ them with their homework. At the weekend, I (6) _____ tennis in the park and (7) _____ dinner for my friends. It was hard work but it was a great life. I (8) _____ to stay in Madrid but I (9) _____ to Manchester to go to university. Happy times!

I hope you're well. Send me an email.

Love,

Reina

P.S. The attachment is a photo of Madrid. Beautiful!

Pronunciation | Past Simple -ed endings

5 a 🔊 36 How is the final *-ed* pronounced in each word? Listen and write /t/, /d/ or /ɪd/.

1 wanted   /ɪd/
2 liked   /t/
3 moved   /d/
4 helped   ___
5 started   ___
6 closed   ___
7 delivered ___
8 cleaned   ___
9 asked   ___
10 stacked ___
11 played   ___
12 cooked   ___

b Listen again and say the words.

6 a 🔊 37 Listen. Complete the sentences with the words you hear.

I *was* in a café yesterday and my phone *was* at home.

1 I _____ to call work.

2 I _____ to a man next to me and I _____ his phone.

3 I _____ work and I _____ to my boss.

4 The guy in the café _____ to my conversation.

5 When I _____ the call, I _____ the man.

6 Then he _____ me a job!

b Listen again. How is the final *-ed* pronounced for each verb?

Vocabulary | money adjectives

1 **a** Put the letters in the correct order to make money adjectives.

opro   *poor*

1 kreob   _____
2 chir   _____
3 name   _____
4 lrecauf with money _____
5 eerusgno   _____
6 seelsrac with money _____

b Complete the dialogues with the adjectives from Exercise 1a.

A: I never buy expensive things.

B: Oh, so you're very *careful with money*.

1 A: I haven't got any money at the moment.
   B: Oh, so you're _____ .
2 A: I never give money to other people and I never buy presents.
   B: Oh, so you're really _____ .
3 A: I've got a lot of money.
   B: Oh, so you're _____ .
4 A: I haven't got any money in the bank and I haven't got a job.
   B: Oh, so you're very _____ .
5 A: I buy expensive presents for my friends and family.
   B: Oh, so you're very _____ .
6 A: I never look at the price of things. I just buy them.
   B: Oh, so you're a bit _____ .

Grammar | Past Simple: negatives and questions

2 Correct the sentences. Use the prompts.

Steve lived in Los Angeles.

He didn't live in Los Angeles.

He lived in Seattle. (Seattle)

1 Our parents worked in a school.
   _____ .
   _____ . (university)
2 We parked in front of the cinema.
   _____ .
   _____ . (theatre)
3 I hated vegetables when I was a child.
   _____ .
   _____ . (fruit)
4 Miriam delivered newspapers when she was a teenager.
   _____ .
   _____ . (magazines)
5 I borrowed €10 from you.
   _____ .
   _____ . (€20)

3 **a** Complete the text with the correct form of the verbs in brackets.

Van Gogh's early life

These days, people pay millions of dollars for Van Gogh's paintings. But it was different in the past. When he was alive, Van Gogh was very poor and people *didn't want* (not want) to buy his paintings. Van Gogh (1) _____ (be) born in The Hague, in Holland in 1853. In 1869 he (2) _____ (start) work. His company, Goupil & Cie, was from Paris. Van Gogh (3) _____ (not move) to Paris but he (4) _____ (not stay) in The Hague. In 1873, he (5) _____ (move) to London. He (6) _____ (be) in love with a woman called Eugenie Loyer but she (7) _____ (not love) him. Van Gogh was very unhappy. He (8) _____ (not like) his job and in 1874 he moved to Paris. But Van Gogh (9) _____ (not stay) in Paris ...

b Write questions and answers about Van Gogh. Use the prompts and the text in exercise 3a.

(Van Gogh/stay/Paris?)

A: *Did Van Gogh stay in Paris?*

B: *No, he didn't.*

1 (Van Gogh/move/London?)
   A: _____ ?
   B: _____ .
2 (Van Gogh/love/Eugenie Loyer?)
   A: _____ ?
   B: _____ .
3 (Eugenie Loyer/love/Van Gogh?)
   A: _____ ?
   B: _____ .
4 (Van Gogh/like/his job?)
   A: _____ ?
   B: _____ .

4 Correct the mistakes.

He didn't wanted to lend me $5.

He didn't want to lend me $5.

1 Did you to work for an international company?

_____ ?

2 My parents move here when I was four years old.

_____ .

3 I didn't earned very much in that job.

_____ ?

4 Was he live in London?

_____ ?

5 Rie was saved €50 a month last year.

_____ .

6 What job did you when you were a teenager?

_____ .

7 Shamal and Yasir didn't to start a new business.

_____ .

8 Who you worked for in Berlin?

_____ ?

Pronunciation | /ɔː/ and /iː/

5 **a** 🌐 38 Listen to the words from the box and complete the table.

> ~~your~~   ~~she~~   four   poor   mean   clean
> three   he   daughter   see   sure   be
> boring   tall

/ɔː/	/iː/
1 *your*	1 *she*
2 _____	2 _____
3 _____	3 _____
4 _____	4 _____
5 _____	5 _____
6 _____	6 _____
7 _____	7 _____

b 🌐 39 Listen and complete the dialogues.

1 **A:** How old is your daughter? Is she _____ ?
   B: No, she isn't. _____ _____ .

2 **A:** The _____ is very _____ .
   B: I know. And the _____ are very _____ .

3 **A:** Sean is _____ _____ .
   B: Are you _____ ? Isn't _____ just
   _____ ?

4 **A:** Did you drink _____ _____ cups of
   _____ ?
   B: No, _____ than _____ !

c Listen again and say the dialogues.

Listening

6 **a** 🌐 40 Cover the audioscript and listen. Match the events (1–6) with the dates (a–f).

Events		Dates	
1	Gauguin was born	a	1855
2	Gauguin moved to Peru	b	1903
3	Gauguin moved back to France	c	1888
4	Gauguin lived with Van Gogh	d	1895
5	Gauguin moved to Tahiti	e	1848
6	Gauguin died	f	1849

b Listen again and answer the questions.

What was Gauguin's full name?

Eugene Henri Paul Gauguin

1 When was Gauguin born?

_____

2 Who did Gauguin move to France with?

_____

3 How long did Gauguin live with Van Gogh?

_____

4 What did Gauguin think of Van Gogh's paintings?

_____

5 What did Gauguin's wife and children do when he moved to Tahiti?

_____

AUDIOSCRIPT

A: This is a painting by Paul Gauguin. His full name was Eugene Henri Paul Gauguin. He was born in Paris on 7th June 1848. His family moved to Peru in 1849.

B: Did they stay in Peru?

A: No, they didn't. In 1855 Gauguin moved back to France with his mother.

B: Was he friends with Van Gogh?

A: An interesting question. He lived with Van Gogh for three months in 1888, but Gauguin didn't like Van Gogh and he didn't like Van Gogh's paintings.

B: When did Gauguin move to Tahiti?

A: He moved there in 1895. His wife and children stayed in Europe. Gauguin didn't want to live in Europe and he loved art from other countries. He worked in Tahiti but it wasn't easy. He wasn't rich. He was very ill and the police in Tahiti even arrested him! He died in 1903.

Vocabulary | high numbers

1 Write the numbers.

2,150

two thousand, one hundred and fifty

1 631

_____

2 1,010

_____

3 980

_____

4 15,612

_____

5 1,200,000

_____

6 86,321

_____

7 115,200

_____

8 200,109

_____

9 9,999

_____

10 5,555,555

_____

2 🔵 41 Listen. Complete the interesting facts with the correct numbers.

1 Mount Everest is *8,850* metres tall.
2 There are more than _____ countries in the world.
3 About _____ people live in the Vatican City.
4 The River Nile in Egypt is _____ kilometres long.
5 Jean Calment died in 1997. She was _____ years old.
6 There are over _____ cars in the world.
7 There are about _____ pandas in China.
8 There are between _____ and _____ languages in the world.
9 The Pacific Ocean is about _____ square kilometres.
10 The average person has between _____ and _____ hairs on their head.

Grammar | Past Simple: irregular verbs

3 **a** Complete the crossword with the Past Simple form of the verbs.

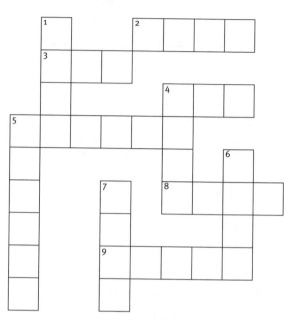

ACROSS	DOWN
2 give	1 come
3 eat	4 go
4 win	5 buy
5 become	6 sell
8 take	7 leave
9 find	

b Complete the sentences with the Past Simple form of the verbs in brackets.

My brother *got* (get) married last year.

1 Oliver and Emma _____ (buy) a house in Spain.
2 We _____ (go) to the cinema last night.
3 I _____ (see) her. She was at the party.
4 Rachel _____ (say) 'no'.
5 My manager and my wife _____ (meet) your daughter yesterday.
6 He _____ (give) me €10 yesterday.
7 Irena and I _____ (find) a beautiful hotel in the centre of Prague.

4 Complete the text with the correct form of the verbs in brackets.

Newly-weds win €15million in Euro Lottery

Janice and Derek Parker from Cornwall _won_ (win) €15 million in the Euro Lottery last week. Janice and Derek (1) _____ (get) married on Saturday morning. 'We (2) _____ (not go) on holiday,' (3) _____ (say) Janice. 'We (4) _____ (not have) any money. But we (5) _____ (go) to a nice restaurant. In the evening, I (6) _____ (look) at the lottery numbers and I (7) _____ (be) so happy.' Last Friday, Derek (8) _____ (buy) a present for Janice. What (9) _____ (he/buy) for her? He (10) _____ (not buy) her a new car or a new house. He (11) _____ (buy) a new washing machine for her!

How to... | talk about questionnaire results

5 Write sentences about the questionnaire results. Use *everyone*, *most people*, *some people* or *no one*.

Question	Yes	No
1 Do you pay by credit card?	40%	60%
2 Do you lend money to friends?	70%	30%
3 Do you borrow money from friends?	35%	65%
4 Do you give a tip?	100%	0%
5 Do you save money every month?	75%	25%
6 Do you invest money in shares?	0%	100%
7 Do you buy things online?	100%	0%

1 _Some people pay by credit card._
2 _Most people lend money to friends._
3 _____ .
4 _____ .
5 _____ .
6 _____ .
7 _____ .

Reading

6 **a** Read the article and complete the table about Alex and Caterina.

	Alex	Caterina
full name:		
nationality:		
websites:		

Internet ideas!

Alex Tew was born in 1984 in the UK. When he was 21 years old, he was a university student and he was broke. Then he had an idea. He started a website called *Million Dollar Homepage*. Alex sold pixels on his website for $1. There were one million pixels on his homepage. Big and small companies bought the pixels. When you click on the pixels, you go to their website.

Alex started the business on 5th August 2005. On 11th January 2006, he sold the last 1,000 pixels on ebay for $38,100. The total income was $1,037,100. Alex was a millionaire.

Caterina Fake was born in Pennsylvania in the USA. She started a website called *Flickr* with her partner, Stewart Butterfield, in 2004. *Flickr* is a photo website. People can put their photos on *Flickr* and other people can see them. In 2005, *Yahoo!* bought *Flickr* for $35 million and Caterina started working for *Yahoo!*. In 2009, she left *Yahoo!* and started a new website called *Hunch*. In 2010, *Hunch. com* had over a million visitors.

b Read the article again and answer the questions.

What was Alex's problem?
He was broke.
1 What did Alex sell?
_____
2 How much money did Alex earn?
_____
3 What can people do on *Flickr*?
_____
4 Who bought *Flickr*?
_____
5 How much did they pay for it?
_____
6 Who did Caterina work for from 2005 to 2009?
_____

Vocabulary | life events

1 Complete the dialogues with the correct verb.

A: Do you like your job?

B: No, I don't. I want to _change_ jobs.

1 A: I joined the gym last week.

B: Oh, do you want to _____ fit?

2 A: Our flat is really small.

B: Do you want to _____ ?

3 A: I've got a car but I can't drive.

B: Do you want to _____ to drive?

4 A: I don't live with my parents now.

B: When did you _____ home?

5 A: What do you want to do when you finish school?

B: I want to _____ a job.

6 A: Pedro isn't at university any more.

B: When did he _____ ?

7 A: Did you _____ in love the first time you met her?

B: Not the first time; maybe the second.

8 A: Do you want to _____ married?

B: Yes, but first I want to _____ someone special.

9 A: Is Mr Larson still with this company?

B: No, he isn't. He was 67 so he decided to _____ .

10 A: Do you like children?

B: Yes, I do. I want to _____ a baby when I'm about 30.

11 A: Do you want to get a job when you finish school?

B: No, I don't. I want to _____ to university.

12 A: My job is really boring.

B: Why don't you _____ your job and _____ your own business?

Grammar | going to: positive

2 Write a sentence for each picture. Use a phrase from Exercise 1a and _going to_.

He's going to learn to drive.

1

_____

2

_____

3

_____

4

_____

5

_____

6

_____

3 Write a second sentence. Use the verbs from the box and *going to*.

> find a new job ~~leave home~~ move
> go to the beach go to bed dance
> cook dinner be rich move to a hot country

He doesn't want to live with his parents any more.
He's going to leave home.

1 This country is cold. I _____ .
2 I went to bed late last night. I _____ early tonight.
3 Estelle doesn't like her job. She _____ .
4 We're on holiday. We _____ this afternoon.
5 He's a good businessman. He _____ .
6 She's a great chef. She _____ tonight.
7 We've got a house in the city but we _____ to the country next year.
8 I love this song. I _____ .

4 Write dialogues. Use the prompts.

(I/retire next year)(my father)
A: *I'm going to retire next year.*
B: *Really? My father's going to retire next year, too.*

(Patricia/quit her job)(Stefan and Romero)
A: *Patricia's going to quit her job.*
B: *Really? Stefan and Romero are going to quit their jobs, too.*

1 (we/have a baby)(my best friend)
A: _____ .
B: _____
_____ .

2 (my sons/go to university)(my daughter)
A: _____ .
B: _____
_____ .

3 (Davina/learn to drive)(I)
A: _____ .
B: _____
_____ .

4 (Mr Ramos/start his own business)(you)
A: _____ .
B: _____
_____ .

5 (I/get fit)(my brother)
A: _____ .
B: _____
_____ .

6 (they/leave home/next month)(we)
A: _____ .
B: _____
_____ .

Reading

5 **a** Read the interviews (A–C) and match them to the pictures (1–3).

A **Congratulations. How do you feel?**
Good. Really good. It was a great night for me.
What are your plans now?
I'm going to go out and celebrate tonight. And then next week I'm going to have a long holiday with my family. We're going to go to South Africa. I just want to swim in the sea and eat out in restaurants. My wife and my children are going to love it and I can't wait. _____

B **Congratulations. How do you feel at the moment?**
Oh, I'm so happy. I can't believe it. This morning I was just a student and now I'm a singer!
What are your plans now?
Well, I'm going to go out and celebrate tonight with my boyfriend. And then tomorrow I'm going to start work on my first album. It's going to be great – number one! _____

C **How do you feel? Are you sad?**
No, not really. I wanted to win but I'm really happy for Jason, too. He's a great actor.
What are your plans now?
Well, tonight I'm just going to go home and have dinner with my wife. But next week I'm going to start work on a new film. It's called *Someone Special*. I play an FBI agent. _____

b Read the interviews again. Complete the sentences with A, B, or C.

C is an actor.
1 ____ is going to change jobs.
2 ____ and ____ are married.
3 ____ and ____ are going to celebrate tonight.
4 ____ and ____ are going to start work again soon.
5 ____ is going to fly to another country.

Vocabulary | emotions

1 **a** Find eight more adjectives of emotion in the word square.

R	M	B	O	R	E	D	B	E
A	A	E	C	L	H	M	D	X
I	N	E	R	V	O	U	S	C
C	G	H	Q	H	M	Z	C	I
K	R	A	L	H	A	U	A	T
L	Y	P	O	A	E	P	R	E
D	E	P	R	E	S	S	E	D
L	Q	Y	L	E	O	E	D	R
F	T	I	R	E	D	T	O	G

b How do you feel? Write sentences with an adjective from exercise 1a.

Your pet cat dies.

I feel depressed.

1 You are in the cinema. It is the first hour of a four hour film. You don't like it.

_____

2 A big present arrives at your door. It is for you.

_____

3 You are going to give a talk to 100 people at work.

_____

4 Some young teenagers write their names in paint on your car.

_____

5 You went to bed late last night and you woke up early this morning.

_____

6 Your manager at work says, 'Well done. You are very good at your job.'

_____

7 Your manager at work says, 'You aren't very good at your job.'

_____

8 You are alone at home in your living room. You hear someone in your kitchen.

_____

Grammar | *going to*: negatives and questions

2 **a** Look at the table about Mel and her family. Write two sentences for each person/people.

	going to	not going to
Mel (me)	eat a lot of vegetables	eat meat
1 my husband	do a lot of exercise	surf the Internet every evening
2 me and my husband	move house	watch a lot of TV
3 my sister	get a new job	go out every night
4 my parents	travel abroad	buy a new car

I'm going to eat a lot of vegetables.

I'm not going to eat meat.

1 He _____

He _____

2 We _____

We _____

3 She _____

She _____

4 They _____

They _____

b Write questions and answers for Mel and her family. Use the prompts and the table.

(you/eat meat)

Are you going to eat meat?

No, I'm not.

(your sister/get a new job)

Is your sister going to get a new job?

Yes, she is.

1 (your parents/buy a new car)

_____ ?

_____ .

2 (your husband/surf the Internet every evening)

_____ .

_____ .

3 (you and your husband/move)

_____ ?

_____ .

4 (your sister/go out every night?)

_____ ?

_____ .

5 (your parents/travel abroad)

_____ ?

_____ .

6 (your husband/do a lot of exercise)

_____ ?

_____ .

3 Complete the dialogue. Use the prompts and the correct form of *going to*.

A: Dad, *I'm going to get married* (I/get married).

B: Married? Who to?

A: James, of course.

B: Well, (1) _____ (I/not pay) for the wedding.

A: Dad! (2) _____ (you/say) 'congratulations'?

B: (3) _____ ? (when/you/get married)

A: In the summer.

B: (4) _____ (we/not be) here. (5) _____ (we/be) on holiday.

A: (6) _____ (you/be) back at the end of July and (7) _____ (we/get) married in August.

B: Oh!

A: (8) _____ (we/not have) a big wedding; just a hundred people.

B: A hundred people? (9) _____ (where/you/ have) the wedding?

A: Here in this house.

B: In my house?

How to... | say goodbye

4 Circle the correct option to complete the dialogues.

A: Bye!

B: *Later see you.* / *See you later.* / *You later see.*

1 A: See you soon.

B: Yes, see you *evening.* / *tomorrow.* / *weekend.*

2 A: Goodbye.

B: *Bye.* / *Good.* / *See.*

3 A: See you on Monday.

B: Yes, have a nice *weekend.* / *tomorrow.* / *Monday.*

4 A: See you tomorrow.

B: Yes, *Have a nice evening.* / *Have a nice holiday.* / *Have a nice weekend.*

Pronunciation | /gəʊɪŋ tə/

5 **a** 🔵 42 Listen and mark the stress.

<u>What</u> are you <u>going</u> to <u>do</u>?

1 Are you going to have a party?

2 Where are you going to live?

3 Is she going to change jobs?

4 Who's going to tell him?

b Listen again and repeat.

Listening

6 **a** 🔵 43 Listen to a story about a fisherman and his grandson. Put the grandson's plans into the correct order.

☐ retire early   ☐ buy a boat

☐ earn a lot of money   `1` go to university

☐ relax   ☐ graduate

☐ start a business

b Listen again. Cover the audioscript and complete the questions with the words you hear.

What are you *going to do* in life?

1 And what _____ after that?

2 What _____ business?

3 What _____ all that money?

4 And _____ with _____ ?

5 How _____ ?

AUDIOSCRIPT

An old fisherman lived in a small house on the beach. He had a little boat and he went fishing in his boat every day. He was poor but he was never angry or upset. One day, the fisherman's grandson came to visit him and they went fishing in the little boat.

'You're a boy now,' said the fisherman, 'but you're going to be a man one day. What are you going to do in life?'

'Grandfather,' said the boy, 'you're a fisherman but you're poor. I don't want to be poor. I'm going to go to university.'

'And what are you going to do after that?' asked the fisherman.

'I'm going to graduate and start a business,' said the boy.

'What sort of business?' asked the fisherman.

'I don't know,' said the boy, 'but I'm going to earn a lot of money.'

'What are you going to do with all that money?' asked the fisherman.

'I'm going to retire early and I'm going to have a lot of free time,' said the boy.

'And what are you going to do with your free time?' asked the fisherman.

'I'm going to relax and enjoy my life,' said the boy.

'How are you going to do that?' asked the fisherman.

The boy thought for a while and then said, 'I'm going to buy a little boat and go fishing every day.'

'Welcome to my world,' said the fisherman.

Grammar | *why* and *because*

1 Put the words in the correct order to make sentences.

late? you Why are
Why are you late?
bus Because come. didn't the
Because the bus didn't come.

1 you upset? Why are
A: _____
I'm Because broke.
B: _____

2 was Why excited? Karen
A: _____
holiday to. booked she a Italy Because
B: _____

3 your sisters Why home? at do live
A: _____
haven't got they money. any Because
B: _____

4 married? get did you Why
A: _____
in Because were love. we
B: _____

5 money? did Why a lot of Henri borrow
A: _____
new Because wanted to car. buy he a
B: _____

2 Correct the mistakes.

Why you want to go home?
Why do you want to go home?

1 I joined the gym because wanted to get fit.
_____ .

2 I bought a new car because my old car awful.
_____ .

3 Why your mother want to move?
_____ .

4 Our cousins didn't to university because they wanted to get a job.
_____ .

5 I sold my CD player I get all my music from the Internet now.
_____ .

6 Why Christine borrow €5?
_____ .

7 Why were late for class yesterday?
_____ .

8 David quit his job because he bored.
_____ .

3 Write dialogues in the Past Simple with *why* and *because*. Use the prompts.

(they/dance all night/good party)
A: *Why did they dance all night?*
B: *Because it was a good party.*

1 (she/cycle up the hill/want to get fit)
A: _____ ?
B: _____ .

2 (he/start playing chess/grandfather was good at it)
A: _____ ?
B: _____ .

3 (he/jump out of the plane/had a parachute)
A: _____ ?
B: _____ .

4 (he/read the book/interesting)
A: _____ ?
B: _____ .

Pronunciation | sentence stress

4 **a** 🔘 44 Listen. <u>Underline</u> the stressed words.

1 A: <u>Why</u> did you <u>buy</u> her a <u>clock</u>?
   B Because she's always late.
2 A: Why did you join the gym?
   B: Because I want to get fit.
3 A: Why did you buy that toy?
   B: Because my sister's going to have a baby.
4 A: Why do you watch so much TV?
   B: Because I like it.

b Listen again and repeat. Copy the stress pattern of the dialogues.

Vocabulary | presents

5 **a** Complete the word puzzle to find the present.

1 You put food on/in these.
2 You buy things with this. It isn't money and it isn't a credit card.
3 You put flowers in this.
4 You play with this.
5 You wear this. It is usually silver or gold.
6 You put a photo in this.
7 You go to the theatre with these.
8 You eat these.
9 You tell the time with this.
10 This is usually green. You give it water.
11 You drink from these.

b Complete the dialogues with words from Exercise 5a.

A: What shall we get him?
B: He loves flowers.
A: I know. Let's get him a _vase_.
1 A: What shall we get her?
   B: She likes silver and gold.
   A: I know. Let's get her some _____ .
2 A: What shall we get them?
   B: They've got a lot of photos of their grandchildren.
   A: I know. Let's get them a _____ .
3 A: What shall we get him?
   B: He loves the theatre.
   A: I know. Let's get him _____ .
4 A: What shall we get her?
   B: She's always late.
   A: I know. Let's get her a _____ .
5 A: What shall we get him?
   B: He loves eating sweet things.
   A: I know. Let's get him some _____ .

How to... | give and receive gifts

6 Complete the dialogues with the words from the box.

> Thank   Oh   You're   These   Don't   ~~This~~

1 A: Here. _This_ is for you.
   B: (1) _____ , that's really kind of you.
   A: (2) _____ welcome.

2 A: (3) _____ are for you.
   B: (4) _____ you. That's really kind of you.
   A: (5) _____ mention it.

The crossword grid (Exercise 5a) spells PLATES ANDBOWLS down the first column with letters: P, L, A, T, E, S, A, N, D, B, O, W, L, S and across clues numbered 1–11, with V, O, U, C, H, E, R, F, O, R, A, S, H, O, P in column 2, and BE U ... D U across the shaded row.

Past Simple

1 Write the Past Simple form of the verbs.

walk _walked_

1 work _____
2 like _____
3 borrow _____
4 live _____
5 look _____
6 clean _____
7 change _____
8 dance _____

2 Complete the sentences with the Past Simple form of the verbs from the box.

> wash   say   borrow   ~~come~~   help   get
> sell   spend   lend

Louise _came_ home at 12 o'clock last night.

1 Cory _____ a new job with PWD Holidays.
2 I _____ all my money on shoes last week.
3 I asked for a three-week holiday but my boss _____ no.
4 My brother _____ me with my homework yesterday evening.
5 Bruno _____ me €50 last week.
6 My father _____ his car on eBay.
7 I _____ $5 because I was broke.
8 Lucy _____ her father's car this morning.

3 Complete the dialogues with the Past Simple form of the verbs in brackets.

A: When _did_ the match _start_? (start)
B: It _started_ at half past three.

1 A: What _____ you _____ for dinner? (have)
   B: I _____ a salad.
2 A: _____ you _____ swimming? (go)
   B: It was cold so we _____ _____ swimming. We _____ to the cinema.
3 A: What _____ you _____ in town? (buy)
   B: I _____ some clothes.
4 A: _____ Marlene _____ any photos of you? (take)
   B: No, she _____ . She _____ some photos of Michael.
5 A: Where _____ Harry and Sally _____ ? (meet)
   B: They _____ at university.
6 A: Where _____ you _____ her? (see)
   B: I _____ her in a café on Trenton Street.
7 A: Oscar _____ home at one o'clock this morning. (come)
   B: Really? What time ____ Liam ____ home?

going to

4 Write sentences with the prompts and the correct form of _going to_.

Stefania/get married
Stefania's going to get married.
I/not move/to another country
I'm not going to move to another country.

1 Samuel/learn to dance
   _____ .
2 Coldplay/not make a new album
   _____ .
3 We/not live in Scotland
   _____ .
4 My son/clean and tidy his room
   _____ .
5 Rie and Alan/not come to the wedding
   _____ .
6 I/not cook dinner
   _____ .
7 You/be late
   _____ .
8 Eleanor/sell her bike
   _____ .

5 Write questions to find extra information.

They're going to move to a new country.
Which country are they going to move to?

1 He's going to buy a car.
   What kind _____ ?
2 I'm going to talk to someone.
   Who _____ ?
3 We're going to meet them tomorrow afternoon.
   What time _____ ?
4 They're going to play sport.
   Which _____ ?
5 He's going to have vegetables for dinner.
   What _____ ?
6 She's going to learn a new language.
   What _____ ?
7 My parents are going to buy a holiday home.
   Where _____ ?

why and *because*

6 Complete the dialogues with a question and an answer. Use the words in brackets.

A: I quit my job.
B: *Why did you quit your job?*
A: *Because I was bored. (bored)*

1 A: Ali is broke.
   B: _____ ?
   A: _____ . (careless with money)

2 A: I didn't help Liana with her homework.
   B: _____ ?
   A: _____ . (tired)

3 A: My dad is going to retire.
   B: _____ ?
   A: _____ . (seventy years old)

4 A: I hate my neighbour.
   B: _____ ?
   A: _____ . (rich but mean)

5 A: I didn't join a gym.
   B: _____ ?
   A: _____ . (expensive)

Vocabulary

7 Complete the sentences with the verbs from the box.

> look   get   meet   invest   work   ~~wash~~
> borrow   leave   deliver   start   lend   win

I'm going to *wash* my dad's car this weekend.

1 Did you _____ all your money in the business?

2 My wife is going to go out tonight. I'm going to _____ after the children.

3 Did you _____ some money on the lottery?

4 Do you _____ full-time or part-time?

5 Don't _____ him any money. He never gives it back.

6 When they leave university, they're going to _____ their own business.

7 I want to _____ a job in a big international company.

8 Did you _____ home when you were eighteen?

9 My son gets up early every morning and _____ newspapers.

10 I'm broke. Can I _____ £10 please?

11 I hope I _____ someone special soon.

8 Write the numbers.

10,301
ten thousand, three hundred and one

1 733
   _____

2 1,140
   _____

3 66,000
   _____

4 112,500
   _____

5 500,105
   _____

6 2,300,630
   _____

9 Choose the correct adjective to complete the sentences.

I haven't got any money. I'm _____ .
a excited   (b broke)   c rich

1 They're going to get married next week. They're really _____ .
   a excited   b generous   c upset

2 He retired last year but he wants to work. Now he's a bit _____ .
   a mean   b nervous   c depressed

3 She buys a lot of presents. She's very _____ .
   a careful with money   b generous   c scared

4 He took my phone and he didn't ask. I'm so _____ .
   a bored   b poor   c angry

5 You never buy expensive things. You're very _____ .
   a careful with money   b careless with money   c excited

6 My exam is tomorrow. I'm a bit _____ .
   a angry   b nervous   c happy

7 I haven't got a lot of money. I'm not very _____ .
   a poor   b depressed   c rich

8 I'm a bit _____ because my teacher was angry with me.
   a upset   b bored   c broke

10 Complete the words to make presents.

ch o c o l a t e s
1 a pl __ nt
2 gl __ ss __ s
3 a v __ s __
4 a ph __ t __ fr __ m __
5 b __ __ __ t __ pr __ d __ cts
6 pl __ t __ s __ nd b __ wls
7 j __ w __ ll __ r __
8 t __ ck __ ts f __ r a sh __ w

Answer key

Unit 1

Lesson 1.1

1
2 computer 3 chocolate 4 taxi 5 telephone 6 pizza 7 doctor
8 bus 9 restaurant 10 television

2a
1 too 2 Hi 3 Welcome 4 My 5 name 6 I'm

2b
B 1 C 4 D 3

3
1 My name's 2 Nice to meet you, too. 3 Thank you. 4 My name's
5 Hello 6 What's your name 7 Nice to meet you 8 I'm

4
B: Hello, Don. I'm Judy.
A: Nice to meet you, Judy.
B: Nice to meet you, too, Don.

5
1 I'm 2 You're 3 I'm 4 I'm

6
1 **A:** Good morning, Mr Nakamura. ~~You~~ in room 9-2-2. **You're**
  B: Thank you. ✓
2 **A:** Hello. ~~Im~~ Jin Chang. **I'm**
  B: ~~Im~~ Farah Coleman. **I'm**
3 **A:** I'm John Wilson. ✓
  B: Hello, Mr Wilson. ~~Youre~~ in room 1-0-2. **You're**

7a
zero, one, two, three, four, five, six, seven, eight, nine, ten

7b

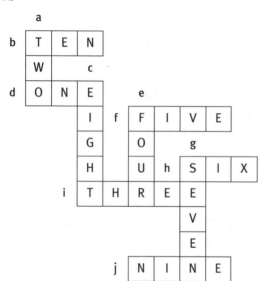

Lesson 1.2

1a
1 China 2 France 3 Germany 4 India 5 Italy 6 Japan 7 Mexico
8 Poland 9 Russia 10 Spain 11 the UK 12 the USA

1b

			5				8	
			P				S	
1			O				P	
B		4	L	6			A	9
R	2	3	M	A	I	7	I	J
A	R	G	E	N	T	I	N	A
Z	U	E	X	D	A	N		P
I	S	R	I		L	D		A
L	S	M	C		Y	I		N
	I	A	O			A		
	A	N						
	Y							

2a
A: Where are you from, Ben?
B: I'm from Poland.
A: Where in Poland?
B: Warsaw.

2b
1 **A:** Where are you from, Kana?
  B: I'm from Japan.
  A: Where in Japan?
  B: Tokyo.
2 **A:** Where are you from, Javier?
  B: I'm from Mexico.
  A: Where in Mexico?
  B: Mexico City.
3 **A:** Where are you from, Ilya?
  B: I'm from Russia.
  A: Where in Russia?
  B: Moscow.

3
1 **A:** Who's she?
  B: She's Amy.
  A: Where's she from?
  B: She's from the UK.
2 **A:** Who's she?
  B: She's Francesca.
  A: Where's she from?
  B: She's from Italy.
3 **A:** Who's he?
  B: He's Calvin.
  A: Where's he from?
  B: He's from the USA.

4
1 She isn't from Spain. She's from India.
2 He isn't from Italy. He's from the USA.
3 She isn't from Russia. She's from Germany.
4 He isn't from Turkey. He's from the UK.

5
1 **A:** Nice computer!
  B: Thanks.
  A: Is it a Dell?
  B: No, it isn't. It's an Apple.
2 **A:** Nice telephone!
  B: Thanks.
  A: Is it a Nokia?
  B: No, it isn't. It's a Motorola.
3 **A:** Nice television.
  B: Thanks.
  A: Is it a Sony?
  B: No, it isn't. It's a Panasonic.

6a
1 Who's he and where's he from?
2 It isn't from Italy. It's from Spain.
3 I'm from Poland and you're from Germany.

7
1 Name: Jane Jones   Room: 6-1-4
2 Name: Paul Earle   Room: 8-1-9
3 Name: Candy Fox   From: Los Angeles in the USA.

Lesson 1.3

1

-ian/an	-ish	-ese
Brazilian	Polish	Chinese
German	Spanish	Japanese
Indian	British	
Italian		
Mexican		
Russian		
American		

2
1 the Brazilian flag   2 the Spanish flag   3 the American flag
4 the Chinese flag   5 the British flag

3
3 My favourite film is *Four Weddings and a Funeral*. It's British.
4 My favourite singer is Lady Gaga. She's American.
5 My favourite actor is Gael Garcia Bernal. He's Mexican.
6 My favourite book is *The Idiot*. It's Russian.
7 My favourite fashion designer is Yamamoto Yohji. He's Japanese.

4
1 oOoo   Brazilian, Italian,
2 Oo   German, Polish, Russian, Spanish
3 Ooo   Mexican
4 oO   Chinese
5 ooO   Japanese

5
1 his   2 your/My   3 Her/your   4 His/your

6
1 What's his name?   2 He's my favourite singer.
3 Who's her favourite actor?   4 What's your favourite food?
5 Her name's Ibis.   6 You're British.

7
1 his   2 you   3 I'm   4 she's   5 he's   6 your   7 My   8 His   9 Her
10 Her   11 My   12 his

Unit 2

Lesson 2.1

1
2 f   3 a   4 c   5 b   6 g   7 d
2
1 h, j, k   2 d, e, g, p, t, v   3 m, n, s, x, z   4 y   5 o   6 u, w   7 r
3
1 AL796SCK   2 Ian Evering   3 Leslie Knight
4
1 **A:** Alan, this is Jon.
   B: Nice to meet you, Jon.
   C: Nice to meet you too, Alan.
2 **A:** Elif, this is Roni.
   B: Nice to meet you, Roni.
   C: Nice to meet you too, Elif.

5
1 **A:** They're Polish.
   B: Where are they from in Poland?
2 **A:** Are we late?
   B: No, we aren't.
3 **A:** Where are they from?
   B: They're from Brazil.
4 **A:** We aren't Spanish. We're Italian.
   B: Are you from Rome?

6
1 **A:** Are Yanni and Petra married?   ✓
   B: No, they are. They're friends.   aren't
2 **A:** Is you and your wife from Moscow?   Are
   B: No, we aren't. Alina's from St Petersburg and I'm from Kazan.   ✓
3 **A:** Your friends are in the garden.   ✓
   B: They not my friends. They're Erica's friends.   They're
4 **A:** Hello. Who is you?   are
   B: I'm Francesca and this is my husband, Tony. We're from Canada.   ✓

7
1 Their   2 They're   3 your   4 You're   5 Our   6 their   7 we're
8
1 Our   2 we're   3 our   4 they're   5 their   6 their   7 your

Lesson 2.2

1

Crossword solution:
3 across WATCH
5 across PURSE
7 across BUSINESS CARD
11 across PEN
12 across PASSPORT
13 across BOOK
15 across UMBRELLA
1 down C...
2 down B...
4 down MOBILEPHONE
6 down TICKET
8 down CAMERA
9 down APLAN...
10 down ORANGE

2

/æ/	/e/
bag	Internet
café	pen
camera	seven
grandpa	umbrella
taxi	

3
1 It's an apple.   2 It's a pen.   3 It's an umbrella.   4 It's a brush.
5 It's an orange.

4
1 **Woman:** Are they televisions?
   Man: No. They aren't televisions. They're computers.
2 **Woman:** Are they mobile phones?
   Man: No. They aren't mobile phones. They're iPods.
3 **Woman:** Are they watches?
   Man: No. They aren't watches. They're mobile phones.

5
Leo
1 an umbrella   2 a brush   3 two apples
Charlie
4 a passport   5 a camera   6 four books   7 two brushes
8 a purse

Lesson 2.3

1
1 f   2 d   3 e   4 j   5 a   6 c   7 b   8 i   9 g   10 h
2
1 fifty-five sixty-six   2 fifty forty   3 twelve eleven
4 seventy-seven eighty-four   5 fifty-four sixty-three
6 sixty-four eighty-one   7 seventy thirty
3
a 30   b 13   c 80   d 19   e 16   f 90   g 40   h 18   i 16

4

1 **A:** How old is he?
  B: He's fifty-two.
2 **A:** How old are you?
  B: I'm twenty-one.
3 **A:** How old are they?
  B: They're eleven and twelve.
4 **A:** How old are you (and your sister)?
  B: We're thirty.

5

1 It isn't/It's not a camera. It's an iPod.
2 We aren't/We're not from the USA. We're from the UK.
3 Paris isn't my favourite country. It's my favourite city.
4 He isn't/He's not my sister. He's my brother.
5 You aren't/You're not fifteen. You're fifty.
6 They aren't/They're not friends. They're cousins.
7 She isn't/She's not an accountant. She's an engineer.

6a

1 are 2 's 3 's 4 Are 5 isn't 6 are 7 Are 8 aren't/'re not 9 're
10 Are 11 are 12 's 13 's

6b

A 3 B 2 C 1

7

1 Name: Derek Age: 65 From: the USA
2 Name: Patricia Age: 68 From: Italy
3 Name: Monica Age: 44 From: France
4 Name: Sam Age: 45 job: teacher
5 Name: Marie Age: 38 job: doctor
6 Name: Malcolm Age: 12 Favourite sport: football
7 Name: Debbie Age: 12 Favourite sport: basketball

Review and consolidation units 1–2

1

1 a 2 c 3 c 4 a 5 c 6 b 7 b 8 c 9 a

2

1 'm 2 Are 3 'm not 4 'm 5 Are 6 aren't/'re not 7 're 8 are 9 're
10 Is 11 isn't/'s not 12 's 13 Is 14 isn't/'s not 15 are

3

1 His 2 your 3 my 4 Their 5 Its 6 her 7 Our

4

1 your 2 my 3 she 4 Her 5 my 6 They're 7 they 8 Their 9 He's

5

1 a 2 – 3 a 4 an 5 – 6 an 7 – 8 – 9 a

6

1 sisters 2 brushes 3 watches 4 cameras 5 oranges

7

1 i 2 f 3 j 4 h 5 g 6 d 7 b 8 c 9 e 10 a

8

1 the UK 2 Italian 3 Russian 4 Japan 5 Chinese 6 French
7 American

9

1 purse 2 ticket 3 book 4 apple 5 mobile phone 6 umbrella
7 orange 8 business card 9 computer

10

1 seventy-nine 2 twenty-three 3 thirteen 4 eight
5 a/one hundred and one 6 twelve 7 fifty-seven 8 fifteen 9 thirty

11

1 father 2 cousin 3 sister 4 daughter 5 husband 6 grandmother
7 brother 8 grandfather 9 mother 10 uncle 11 aunt

Unit 3

Lesson 3.1

1

1	C	I	N	E	M	A				
		2	C	A	F	É				
	3	B	A	N	K					
		4	C	A	S	H	P	O	I	N	T
5	C	L	O	T	H	E	S	S	H	O	P
	6	S	U	P	E	R	M	A	R	K	E	T
	7	B	U	S	S	T	O	P			
8	R	E	S	T	A	U	R	A	N	T	
9	S	H	O	E	S	H	O	P			
10	C	A	R	P	A	R	K				

2

1 Luka's parents are from Italy.
2 Sandra's favourite drink is coffee.
3 Luka's children are three and five.
4 Sandra's sons are twelve and fifteen.

3

1 **A:** Where are Grace's parents from?
  B: They're from Argentina.
2 **A:** What's Leo's surname?
  B: It's Webber.
3 **A:** Where are Elif's parents from?
  B: They're from Turkey.
4 **A:** Who is Valentina's best friend?
  B: It's Catalina.
5 **A:** How old are Sem's children.
  B: They're three and five.

4

1 What is your sister's favourite snack?
2 What is Vladimir's surname?
3 My child's favourite food is cheese.
4 Her children's favourite food is chocolate.
5 That's my mother's favourite film.

5

1 P 2 P 3 l 4 P 5 P 6 l 7 P

6

1 b coffee c water
2 a coffee b salad c juice
3 a sandwich b chocolate cake c tea

7a

1 a 2 b 3 a 4 b 5 c 6 b 7 a

8

1 have 2 away 3 else 4 please 5 sugar 6 No

Lesson 3.2

1

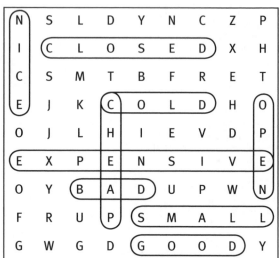

2a
1 big 2 expensive 3 fast 4 closed 5 cold

2b
1 big – small 2 expensive – cheap 3 fast – slow 4 closed – open
5 cold – hot

3
1 open 2 cold 3 old 4 fast 5 free 6 fresh 7 nice

4a
1 Hel<u>lo</u>. Is this <u>Joe's hotel</u>? 2 <u>So</u>, is this your cl<u>o</u>thes shop?
3 <u>Oh</u>, n<u>o</u>! My computer is s<u>o</u> sl<u>ow</u>.

5
1 a Is your salad good?   b Is it a good salad?
2 a Are the sandwiches fresh? b Are they fresh sandwiches?
3 a Her phone is expensive.   b It's an expensive phone.
4 a They are nice apples.   b The apples are nice.

6
1 The shoe shop is closed.
2 This salad is really nice.
3 Can I have a big piece of chocolate cake?
4 Your sandwiches are small.
5 They aren't expensive.
6 It's a very nice deli.
7 That's a really expensive car.

7
1 It's in London. 2 No, it isn't. 3 They're from Italy. 4 It's free.
5 Luis and Camilla. 6 Luis is from Spain and Camilla is from the UK.
7 They're/It's about £80 for one night.

Lesson 3.3

1a
1 That's two dollars <u>forty-five</u>, please.
2 That's fifty <u>cents</u>, please.
3 That's six <u>pounds</u> twenty-nine, please.
4 That's three euros sixty cents, please.
5 That's ninety-nine <u>cents</u>, please.
6 That's eleven <u>euros</u> forty-nine, please.
7 That's eighty <u>pence</u>, please.

1b
1 The shoes are seventy-five euros ninety-nine.
2 The camera is six euros twenty-nine.
3 The bag is twenty-four pounds sixty.
4 The books are four dollars fifty.
5 The mobile phone is eighty-nine dollars ninety-nine.

2a
1 That's 2 Here 3 Here's 4 altogether 5 That's 6 pay 7 number

2b
1 That's three pounds fifty, please.
2 Can I pay by card?
3 Sure. Enter your PIN number, please.
4 Here's your card and your receipt.

3
1 a 2 b

4
1 That bag is €24. 2 Is this your suitcase? 3 Are those shoes new?
4 These shops are closed today. 5 This is my brother, Clive.
6 Those chocolates are expensive. 7 How much is that computer?

5
1 white 2 orange 3 green 4 blue 5 black 6 yellow 7 red

6
1 The Spanish flag is red and yellow.
2 The Argentinean flag is blue and white.
3 The Polish flag is white and red.
4 The German flag is black, red and yellow.
5 The Brazilian flag is green, yellow and blue.

7
1 a black purse 2 €14.99 3 card
4 green apples 5 £1.99 a kilo (£4.20 in total) 6 cash
7 a blue camera 8 $55.99 9 card

Unit 4

Lesson 4.1

1a
1 airp<u>or</u>t 2 g<u>a</u>llery 3 mus<u>eu</u>m 4 river 5 the<u>a</u>tre 6 nati<u>o</u>nal park
7 the se<u>a</u> 8 be<u>a</u>ch 9 l<u>a</u>ke 10 m<u>a</u>rket 11 mo<u>u</u>ntain

1b
1 gallery 2 lake 3 market 4 museum 5 mountain

2a
1 nice 2 OK 3 not very good 4 awful

2b
1 She's fantastic. 2 He's OK. 3 She's terrible. 4 She's good.

3
1 I think New York is a great city.
2 I don't think those shops are very good.
3 I think Francis is my best friend/my best friend is Francis.
4 I don't think the market is very expensive.

4
1 there are 2 There's 3 there's 4 There are 5 there's 6 There's
7 there are 8 There's 9 There's 10 There are

5
Suggested answers: 1 some 2 a lot of 3 a lot of 4 some 5 some

6
1 There are some 2 There's a 3 There are a lot of
4 there are also a lot of 5 There are some 6 There are about 100
7 There's a 8 There are some

Lesson 4.2

1

I	A	G	B	U	R	F	S
N	E	X	T	T	O	D	U
F	X	U	N	L	O	O	N
R	C	O	N	Z	A	H	D
O	P	P	O	S	I	T	E
N	M	P	J	S	N	Y	R
T	Q	N	E	A	R	U	H
O	A	L	K	D	G	M	B
F	D	G	E	K	I	Y	W

2
1 opposite 2 in front of 3 under 4 next to 5 near

3
1 **A:** Is there a cinema in this shopping centre?
    B: No, there isn't.
2 **A:** Are there any shoe shops in this shopping centre?
    B: No, there aren't.
3 **A:** Are there any bookshops in this shopping centre?
    B: Yes, there are.
4 **A:** Is there a car park in this shopping centre?
    B: Yes, there is.

4
1 There's a restaurant. 2 There's a supermarket.
3 There aren't any shoe shops. 4 There isn't a train station.
5 There are two bookshops. 6 There aren't any museums.
7 There's a clothes shop. 8 There isn't a cinema.

5
1 near 2 there 3 Excuse 4 is 5 Are 6 are 7 Thank 8 welcome
9 Is 10 there

6a

		/θ/	/ð/
1	that		✓
2	three	✓	
3	mother		✓
4	these		✓
5	thirty	✓	
6	thank	✓	
7	there		✓
8	theatre	✓	
9	those		✓
10	brother		✓
11	they		✓

7

1 Are there any museums or galleries near here?
2 Is there a chemist near here?
3 Are there any cafés or restaurants near here?

8

a café b hotel c restaurant d chemist e hotel

Lesson 4.3

1

1 half past six/six thirty 2 ten to ten/nine fifty
3 twenty past eleven/eleven twenty 4 one o'clock
5 half past eight/eight thirty 6 quarter past six/six fifteen
7 twenty-five to six/five thirty-five 8 five past five/five oh five

2

1 **A:** Excuse me. What's the time, please?
  B: It's twenty past seven/seven twenty.
  A: And what time is the train to Izmit?
  B: It's at twenty-five to eight/seven thirty-five.
2 **A:** Excuse me. What's the time, please?
  B: It's five to ten/nine fifty-five.
  A: And what time is the train to Kazan?
  B: It's at half past ten/ten thirty.

3

1 3:30 2 1:40 3 10:10 4 7:35

4a

B: (1) That's £13.50, please.
A: (2) Here you are.
B: (3) Thank you.
A: (4) What time is the next train?
B: (5) It's at 10:35.
A: (6) And what platform is it on?
B: (7) It's on platform one.

4b

B: That's €5.10, please.
A: Here you are.
B: Thank you.
A: What time is the next train?
B: It's at 9:50.
A: And what platform is it on?
B: It's on platform three.

5a and b

1 theatre 2 river 3 under 4 opposite 5 London 6 station

6a

1 Is there a big river in London? (3)
· 2 What's the time? Is it seven o'clock? (3)

7

name	National Railway Museum	Money Museum	Museum of Bad Art (MOBA)
city	York	Colorado Springs	Dedham
opening times	10a.m.–6p.m.	10.30a.m.–5p.m.	2p.m.–9p.m.
cost	free/car park £9/day	$5 for adults	free
there is/are	over 100 trains, a lot of art, a restaurant, a café, a gift shop and a car park	coins and paper money, a dollar from 1804 and a gift shop	over 400 pieces of bad art (and a café upstairs)

Review and consolidation units 3–4

1

1 Who's Fiona's sister? 2 Where are the girls' passports?
3 Are they Oliver's shoes? 4 What's Jennifer's email address?
5 Where are your parents' bags? 6 Who's Harvey's cousin?
7 Are you Leah's brother?

2

1 b 2 a 3 a 4 b 5 b

3

1 those 2 that 3 this 4 These 5 that 6 that 7 these

4

1 there is 2 are there 3 there are 4 There's 5 there's 6 Are there
7 there are 8 There's 9 there are 10 is there 11 there isn't
12 Are there 13 there aren't 14 Is there 15 there is

5

1 some 2 a lot of 3 any 4 a lot of 5 any

6

1 expensive 2 gallery 3 fantastic 4 cold 5 cheese sandwich
6 purple 7 bus stop

7

2 d 3 g 4 a 5 h 6 c 7 e 8 b

8

1 in front of 2 under 3 near 4 next to 5 in 6 opposite

9

1 It's eleven o'clock. 2 It's half past four/four thirty.
3 It's quarter past five/five fifteen. 4 It's twenty to nine/eight forty.
5 It's ten past eleven/eleven ten. 6 It's five past nine/nine oh five.
7 It's quarter past one/one fifteen.
8 It's twenty-five to nine/eight thirty-five. 9 It's half past six/six thirty.

Unit 5

Lesson 5.1

1a

1b

1a short 1b tall 2a old 2b young 3a fair 3b dark

2

1 work for 2 live 3 work in 4 have 5 live in 6 work as 7 live with

3a

1 I like rock music. 2 I don't like football. 3 I like computers.
4 I don't like Indian food. 5 I don't like James Bond films.
6 I like children.

3b

1 **A:** Do you live with your parents?
  B: No, I don't.
2 **A:** Do you have any brothers or sisters?
  B: Yes, I do.
3 **A:** Do you work for a big company?
  B: No, I don't.
4 **A:** Do you live in Mexico City?
  B: Yes, I do.
5 **A:** Do you work in a school?
  B: Yes, I do.

4a

1 /uː/ new, students, two, who, you
2 /əʊ/ euro, go, oh, so, those

5a

			/uː/	/əʊ/
1	What is there to do in Vancouver?		3	0
2	Those two new students are so nice.		3	2

6a

1 a shame 2 see

6b

1 Oh, I see. 2 Really? That's great!

7a

John is an actor. Larry works for a big bank.

7b

1 have 2 wife 3 Sorry 4 work 5 What 6 do 7 for

Lesson 5.2

1a
1 d 2 b 3 a 4 d 5 c 6 a 7 b

1b
1 have a shower 2 start work 3 finish work 4 watch TV 5 go to bed

2
1 She has a shower at 10:45. 2 She starts work at 11:30.
3 She finishes work at 5:00. 4 She watches TV at 6:00.
5 She goes to bed at 2:30 in the morning.

3
1 William doesn't start work early.
2 He doesn't watch TV with his daughter.
3 Irene doesn't have a shower every day.
4 Ricky doesn't make dinner for his children.

4
1 No, she doesn't. 2 Yes, she does. 3 No, she doesn't.
4 Yes, she does. 5 No, she doesn't.

5a
A 3 B 1 C 2

5b
1 Lin 2 Lin 3 Claudia and Olivia 4 Claudia 5 Olivia 6 Claudia and Lin

6a

/s/	/z/	/ɪz/
eats	does	finishes
gets	goes	watches
likes	lives	
starts		

Lesson 5.3

1a
1 Monday 2 Tuesday 3 Wednesday 4 Thursday 5 Friday
6 Saturday 7 Sunday

1b
1 in 2 at/on 3 in/at 4 on/on

2
1 study a language 2 stay at home 3 surf the Internet
4 make friends 5 say hello 6 call your friends 7 play sport

3

1	M	A	K	E	F	R	I	E	N	D	S			
	I													
2	S	A	Y	H	E	L	L	O						
3	S	T	A	Y	A	T	H	O	M	E				
	I													
4	S	U	R	F	T	H	E	I	N	T	E	R	N	E	T
5	S	T	U	D	Y	A	L	A	N	G	U	A	G	E
	I													
6	P	L	A	Y	S	P	O	R	T					
	P													
	I													

4
1 **Grace:** We don't play sport. They play sport at the weekend.
2 **Grace:** They eat in restaurants on Friday and Saturday evenings.
   We don't eat in restaurants.
3 **Grace:** We like our jobs. They don't like their jobs.
4 **Grace:** We get up early. They don't get up early.

5
1 do/do 2 do/like 3 like 4 don't like 5 do/like 6 do/like 7 don't
8 like

6a
1 What 2 Where 3 When 4 How 5 What 6 Who 7 What 8 What

6b
1 Where do you live? 2 What do you do? 3 What do you teach?
4 When/What time do you start work? 5 Who do you live with?

7a
1 <u>Where</u> do you <u>live</u>? 2 <u>Who</u> do you <u>like</u>? 3 <u>When</u> do you <u>go</u> to <u>bed</u>?
4 <u>What</u> do you <u>do</u>?

Unit 6

Lesson 6.1

1
1 kitchen 2 cellar 3 loft 4 bathroom 5 bedroom 6 garden 7 hall
8 garage 9 living room

2
1 basin 2 cooker 3 fridge 4 coffee table 5 wardrobe 6 sink
7 washing machine 8 armchair 9 bath 10 toilet 11 mirror

3
Bathroom: basin bath toilet
Bedroom: mirror wardrobe
Kitchen: cooker fridge sink washing machine
Living room: armchair coffee table

4a
1 's got 2 hasn't got 3 've got 4 haven't got 5 've got

4b
1 's got 2 hasn't got 3 's got 4 hasn't got 5 hasn't got

5
1 have 2 Have, got 3 haven't 4 Has, got 5 has 6 's got

6
1 Ravi's got a new house.
2 My parents haven't got a washing machine.
3 **A:** Has your house got a garage?
   B: No, it hasn't.
4 **A:** Has that hotel got a swimming pool?
   B: Yes, it has.
5 My hotel room hasn't got a bath.
6 We've got a new baby.
7 You've got a beautiful flat.
8 My sisters haven't got any children.
9 **A:** Have we got any milk in the fridge?
   B: Yes, we have.

7a
1 Oscar 2 Oscar's friends 3 Rink's cousin 4 Oscar's friends 5 Rink
6 Oscar's friends

7b
1 It's the main street in St Petersburg.
2 There are a lot of shops and restaurants. 3 It's 500 years old.
4 Copacabana Beach, Sugarloaf Mountain and Carnival.
5 He's a singer.

Lesson 6.2

1a
1 a 2 c 3 c 4 c 5 b 6 a 7 b 8 b

1b
A iron the clothes B clean the bathroom C do the laundry
D vacuum the stairs E wash the dishes F lay the table
G sweep the floor

2a
1 **A:** Can you wash the dishes, please?
   B: Yes, of course.
2 **A:** Can you sweep the floor, please.
   B: No, I can't. I'm sorry. I'm late.

2b
1 **A:** Can you carry my bags, please?
   B: Yes, of course.
2 **A:** Can you answer the phone, please.
   B: No, I'm sorry. I can't.

3a

100%	always
↑	usually
	sometimes
0%	never

3b
1 I <u>always</u> wash the dishes.
2 She <u>sometimes</u> does the laundry.
3 My children <u>never</u> tidy their bedrooms.
4 The food in that restaurant is <u>usually</u> terrible.
5 I <u>sometimes</u> make breakfast for my wife on Sunday.
6 He is <u>always</u> happy on Friday afternoons.
7 I <u>never</u> go to the gym before work.
8 Our cleaner is <u>usually</u> really fast.

4

1 Maggie <u>usually</u> plays sport on Friday afternoon.
2 I sometimes <u>i</u>ron her clothes.
3 You <u>are</u> sometimes really sad.
4 <u>He</u> never finishes work late on Friday.
5 Her friends are <u>always</u> attractive.
6 British people ~~are~~ usually have a sandwich for lunch.

5a

1 /ɪ/   2 /ʌ/   3 /ɪ/

5b

1 Is my d<u>i</u>nner in the k<u>i</u>tchen?
2 I l<u>o</u>ve S<u>u</u>ndays b<u>u</u>t I hate M<u>o</u>ndays.
3 Where's his b<u>u</u>siness card? It's <u>i</u>n the l<u>i</u>v<u>i</u>ng room.

6

1 Ron   2 Per   3 Matthew   4 Felipe   5 Ron

Lesson 6.3

1

1 I'd like   2 Would you like   3 Would you like   4 Yes, please
5 What would you like   6 I'd like

2a

1 Would <u>you</u> like something to eat?   2 What would <u>you</u> like to drink?
3 Would <u>you</u> like a cold drink?

2b

1 Would you like an orange juice?
2 What would you like in your sandwich?
3 Would you like a hot drink?
4 Would you like a snack?

3

1 like   2 want   3 like   4 like   5 want   6 like   7 want   8 like

4

1 working   2 finishing   3 to start   4 to go   5 working   6 to be
7 making   8 living   9 to talk

5a

a a stereo   b a flat-screen TV   c a laptop   d a camera   e a camcorder
f a games console

5b

1 play   games console   2 take   camcorder   3 watch   flat-screen TV
4 surf   laptop   wireless Internet   5 take   camera   6 watch   DVD player

6

1 orange cheesecake   2 a nice stereo   3 a laptop, an old games console
4 a laptop   5 a new games console   6 listening to music
7 listening to music and playing computer games

Review and consolidation units 5–6

1

1 like   2 watch   3 doesn't eat   4 doesn't say   5 doesn't like   6 finish
7 finishes   8 stay   9 loves   10 calls

2

1 **A:** Do your sisters like your wife?   **B:** No, they don't.
2 **A:** Does Jibril eat a lot?   **B:** Yes, he does.
3 **A:** Do they work from home?   **B:** Yes, they do.
4 **A:** Does Felix love her?   **B:** No, he doesn't.
5 **A:** Do your friends live in Barcelona?   **B:** Yes, they do.
6 **A:** Does Ramzi go to bed early?   **B:** No, he doesn't.
7 **A:** Do we have any food in the house?   **B:** No, we don't.

3

1 Where do you live?   2 What do you do?
3 How do you say hello in German?   4 Who do you work for?
5 What time do you get up?   6 What languages do you study?
7 When does the party start?   8 Who does Mirina live with?

4

1 've got   2 Has, got   3 hasn't   4 haven't got   5 Have, got   6 haven't
7 have got   8 've got   9 Have, got   10 have   11 Has, got   12 has
13 has, got   14 's got   15 've got   16 Have, got   17 haven't

5

1 I'm usually late.   2 Do you sometimes work from home?
3 Are they always happy?   4 I usually have a coffee in the morning.
5 Do you sometimes make dinner?   6 She is never late.
7 They never clean the bathroom.
8 We always get up before 9 o'clock at the weekend.

6

1 My sister doesn't like doing the laundry.
2 Sol and Kay don't want to go swimming.
3 Alan likes playing football.
4 Teachers don't like finishing work late.
5 I don't want to make dinner tonight.
6 Tom wants to meet Penelope.
7 Do you like playing sport?
8 Ewa and Adam like watching TV.

7

1 stay at home   2 play sport   3 go to bed   4 finish work
5 empty the dishwasher   6 make dinner   7 say hello   8 do the laundry

8

1 d   2 b   3 b   4 d   5 a   6 c   7 a   8 c   9 c   10 c

Unit 7

Lesson 7.1

1a

1 puzzles   2 aerobics   3 a walk   4 cycling   5 chess   6 a gallery
7 exercise

1b

play chess, tennis
do puzzles, aerobics, exercise
go for a walk
go to a gallery
go cycling

2a

1 don't mind   2 loves   3 doesn't like   4 hate   5 quite likes

2b

1 **Olive:** 'I don't mind going to galleries but Bella hates it.'
2 **Bella:** 'I quite like Twitter but Olive doesn't like it.'
3 **Olive:** 'I hate staying at home on a Saturday night but Bella likes it.'
4 **Bella:** 'I don't mind doing puzzles but Olive loves it.'
5 **Olive:** 'I quite like sushi but Bella doesn't like it.'

3a

1 sure   2 Let's / Yes   3 Why / nice

3b

1 **A:** Let's do a puzzle.   **B:** I'm not sure. I'm quite busy.
2 **A:** Why don't we play tennis?   **B:** OK. That sounds nice.
3 **A:** Shall we go for a walk?   **B:** Yes, OK.

4a

1 eight   2 bike   3 mind   4 play   5 take

4b

1 /eɪ/   2 /aɪ/   3 /aɪ/   4 /eɪ/   5 /eɪ/

5a

1 Do you hate pl<u>ay</u>ing tennis?   2 I don't m<u>i</u>nd getting up at <u>eigh</u>t.

6a

1 us   2 her   3 him   4 you   5 them

6b

1 me   2 you   3 us   4 him   5 them   6 it   7 her

Lesson 7.2

1a

2 e   3 f   4 h   5 b   6 a   7 g   8 i   9 d

1b

1 play the piano   2 use a computer   3 drive a car   4 cook dinner
5 talk to animals   6 speak French   7 dance the tango

2

1 Jim and Jane can cook but they can't drive.
2 Ibrahim can swim but he can't use a computer.
3 We can't play chess but we can play the piano.
4 Jing can use a computer but she can't write computer programmes.
5 We can't drive but we can dance.

3

1 I can   2 They can   3 Can you   4 can   5 I can't   6 he can   7 Can he
8 he can't

4a

1 My brother, Eddie, can't drive but my parents can.
2 My brother, Eddie can swim but I can't.
3 My sister, Jo, can't sing but my brother, Eddie, can.

4b

1 **A:** Can your parents use a computer?
  B: No, they can't.
2 **A:** Can your sister play the piano?
  B: No, she can't.
3 **A:** Can you dance?
  B: Yes, I can.

5a

1 I can't dance the tango.
2 My friend can write computer programs.
3 Some people can talk to animals.
4 Can he sing and dance?
5 We can't use a computer.

6

1 Men and Women.   2 He thinks that they are different.
3 She's a writer (too).   4 The Male mind and the Female Mind.
5 She thinks that they are the same.

Lesson 7.3

1a

January, February, March, April, May, June, July, August, September,
October, November, December

1b

1 July 2 January 3 August 4 February 5 September 6 December
7 May 8 June 9 October 10 March 11 November

2

3

1 1st May   2 the twelfth of December   3 20th June   4 16th November
5 the second of September   6 the third of February   7 12th October
8 the thirtieth of April   9 9th July

4

1 on 2 at 3 on 4 on 5 at 6 in 7 at 8 on 9 in

5

1 Does your new job start at the beginning of April?
2 Is the show sold out at the end of June?
3 Do you want to go out on Friday evening?
4 Shall we go to the theatre on 3rd March?
5 Is her birthday in June?
6 Does the film start at half past seven?

6a

1 B 2 A 3 C

6b

	what?	when?	why not?
1	go to the theatre	19th April	sister's birthday
2	go on holiday to Scotland	8th–15th July	brother's birthday
3	trip to the beach	29th August	

Unit 8

Lesson 8.1

1

1 two thousand and four 2 eighteen oh three 3 nineteen oh nine
4 nineteen seventy 5 two thousand and twelve
6 eighteen eighty-one 7 nineteen ninety-nine
8 two thousand and fifteen

2a and b

1 Date: 21st December 1913
   Other information: 'Word-cross'
2 Date: 3rd April 1973
   Other information: New York.
3 Date: 28th April 2001
   Other information: Dennis Tito.

3a

1 politician 2 scientist 3 singer 4 writer 5 musician
6 business person 7 actor 8 artist 9 dancer 10 leader

3b

4

1 was 2 were 3 was 4 was 5 was 6 were 7 was 8 were 9 were
10 was 11 were 12 was 13 was 14 were

5

1 My son and daughter were at home.   2 I was a singer.
3 You were my best friend.   4 They were at school.
5 She was a teacher in Australia.

6

1 a and d 2 b and c 3 a and c 4 b and d

7a

1 The first president of the USA 2 The first billionaire
3 The first World Cup 4 The first Internet celebrity

7b

1 T 2 F 3 T 4 F 5 T 6 T 7 T

Lesson 8.2

1a

B, A, E, D, C

1b

1 yesterday 2 in 3 last 4 ago 5 on 6 last 7 ago 8 yesterday
9 last 10 in

2a

1 Her parents weren't born in the UK. They were born in the USA and
   Australia.
2 She wasn't a good singer at school. She was a good actor.
3 She wasn't an English student at University. She was an Economics
   student.
4 Her first big film wasn't *Elizabeth I*. It was *Oscar and Lucinda*.
5 Roman wasn't born in 2003. He was born in 2004.

2b

1 Were her parents born in the UK?
  No, they weren't.
2 Was she a good singer at school?
  No, she wasn't.
3 Was she an English student at university?
  No, she wasn't.
4 Was her first big film *Elizabeth I*?
  No, it wasn't.
5 Was Roman born in 2003?
  No, he wasn't.

3

1 were 2 wasn't 3 was 4 were 5 were 6 were 7 were 8 were
9 was 10 Were 11 weren't 12 was 13 was

4

1 Richard and Alex <u>weren't</u> at work yesterday.
2 <u>Was</u> your father a politician?
3 <u>Was</u> Ronald Reagan a film star?
4 My father <u>wasn't</u> a singer but he was a musician.
5 <u>Were</u> you at home last night?
6 When <u>was</u> your last holiday?
7 Who <u>was</u> your best friend was at school?
8 What <u>was</u> Marlon Brando's last film?

5a

1 b 2 c 3 b 4 a

5b

1 Roll 2 again 3 mind 4 win 5 done

Lesson 8.3

1a

1 flight 2 date 3 trip 4 weekend

1b

1 flight / awful 2 date / attractive 3 weekend / Fine
4 holiday / fantastic

2

1 I want to go to <u>town</u> <u>now</u> to buy some <u>flowers</u>.
2 <u>How</u> tall is that <u>mountain</u>? <u>About</u> two <u>thousand</u> metres?
3 <u>Mouse</u> is a <u>noun</u> but <u>how</u> do you <u>pronounce</u> it?

3a

1 far 2 deep 3 heavy 4 long 5 wide

3b

1 far 2 heavy 3 deep 4 long 5 wide

4a and b

How old is the Taj Mahal in India?   a
1 How far is New York from London/London from New York?   c
2 How deep is the Mariana Trench in the Pacific Ocean?   a
3 How tall was Napoleon?   c
4 How long is Route 66 in the USA?   b
5 How wide is the Grand Canyon?   a
6 How tall is Mount Fuji in Japan?   b
7 How long is Ayers Rock in Australia?   c

5a

1 In Chicago 2 She was a sales assistant 3 It's a shop
4 About two years 5 Three 6 About three years old

5b

1 fine 2 was 3 wasn't 4 that 5 questions 6 old

Review and consolidation units 7–8

1

1 you 2 them 3 it 4 me 5 her 6 us 7 him

2

1 Jovita can't do aerobics. 2 They can speak Spanish.
3 Can you use a computer? 4 Your brothers can sing and dance.
5 My husband can't cook. 6 Can your son write computer programmes?
7 People can't talk to animals. 8 Can your parents play the piano?

3

1 Your children can do puzzles but they can't play the piano. Can
  they play chess?
2 You can speak French but you can't cook French food. Can you
  read French books?
3 Mimi can use a computer but she can't write computer
  programmes. Can she play computer games?

4

1 A: Is the party <u>on</u> Friday?
  B: No, it isn't. It's <u>on</u> Saturday.
2 A: Does Ramadan start <u>at</u> the beginning of August this year?
  B: No, it doesn't. It starts <u>at</u> the end of July.
3 A: She was born <u>in</u> 2005.
  B: No she wasn't. She was born <u>at</u> the end of 2004.
4 A: Do you start your new job <u>on</u> 21st March?
  B: No, I don't. I start it <u>on</u> 28th March.
5 A: The match starts <u>at</u> 3:30.
  B: No, it doesn't. It starts <u>at</u> 3pm.

5

1 was 2 were 3 were 4 was 5 was 6 was 7 Was 8 wasn't 9 was
10 Were 11 weren't 12 was 13 was 14 were

6

1 What were their names? 2 Was he a teacher?
3 Where was she yesterday? 4 When was your birthday?
5 How was your holiday? 6 Was he your best friend?
7 Were they good friends?

7

1 How long was your flight? 2 How deep is the swimming pool?
3 How was the party? 4 How far is her house? 5 How was your date?
6 How heavy is your bag? 7 How wide is her garden?

8

1 b 2 b 3 c 4 b 5 c 6 a 7 c 8 b

9

1 It's the eleventh of March, nineteen ninety-five.
2 It's the thirty-first of December.
3 It's the first of January.
4 It's the twentieth of September.
5 It's on the tenth of June.
6 It's the eighth of April, two thousand and nine.

10

1 He's a singer. 2 They're writers. 3 She's a business person.
4 He's a musician. 5 They're scientists. 6 She's an actor.
7 They're artists. 8 They're sports stars. 9 She's a politician.

Unit 9

Lesson 9.1

1

1 pay 2 earn 3 borrow 4 buy 5 spend 6 save 7 sell 8 win 9 invest

2a

2 h 3 e 4 a 5 b 6 d 7 c 8 f

2b

1 help your brother with his homework 2 stack shelves
3 look after your neighbours' children 4 clean and tidy at home
5 deliver newspapers 6 work part-time 7 wash cars

3

1 My sister helped me with my homework
2 He invested all his money in shares
3 I borrowed money from my parents
4 My friends stacked shelves in a supermarket
5 We worked nights in a factory
6 I washed my father's car
7 That boy delivered our newspapers
8 He saved all his money. He hated spending it

4

1 lived 2 started 3 cleaned 4 looked 5 helped 6 played 7 cooked
8 wanted 9 moved

5a

4 /t/ 5 /ɪd/ 6 /d/ 7 /d/ 8 /d/ 9 /t/ 10 /t/ 11 /d/ 12 /t/

6a and b

1 needed /ɪd/ 2 talked /t/ / borrowed /d/ 3 called /d/ / talked /t/
4 listened /d/ 5 finished /t/ / thanked /t/ 6 offered /d/

Lesson 9.2

1a

1 broke 2 rich 3 mean 4 careful with money 5 generous
6 careless with money

1b

1 broke 2 mean 3 rich 4 poor 5 generous 6 careless with money

2
1 They didn't work in a school. They worked in a university.
2 We didn't park in front of the cinema. We parked in front of the theatre.
3 I didn't hate vegetables when I was a child. I hated fruit.
4 She didn't deliver newspapers when she was a teenager. She delivered magazines.
5 I didn't borrow €10 from you. I borrowed €20.

3a
1 was 2 started 3 didn't move 4 didn't stay 5 moved 6 was
7 didn't love 8 didn't like 9 didn't stay

3b
1 **A:** Did Van Gogh move to London?
  B: Yes, he did.
2 **A:** Did Van Gogh love Eugenie Loyer?
  B: Yes, he did.
3 **A:** Did Eugenie Loyer love Van Gogh?
  B: No, she didn't.
4 **A:** Did Van Gogh like his job?
  B: No, he didn't.

4
1 Did you ~~to~~ work for an international company?
2 My parents moved here when I was four years old.
3 I didn't ~~earned~~ very much in that job.
4 ~~Was~~ Did he live in London?
5 Rie ~~was~~ saved €50 a month last year.
6 What job did you ~~do~~ when you were a teenager?
7 Shamal and Yasir didn't ~~to~~ start a new business.
8 Who ~~did~~ you ~~worked~~ for in Berlin?

5a

/ɔː/		/ɪː/	
1	your	1	she
2	four	2	mean
3	poor	3	clean
4	daughter	4	three
5	sure	5	he
6	boring	6	see
7	tall	7	be

5b
1 four/She's three 2 sea/clean/trees/green
3 really poor/sure/he/mean 4 three free/coffee/more/four

6a
1 e 2 f 3 a 4 c 5 d 6 b

6b
1 7th June, 1848 **2** with his mother **3** three months
4 he didn't like them **5** they stayed in Europe

Lesson 9.3

1
1 six hundred and thirty-one
2 one/a thousand and ten
3 nine hundred and eighty
4 fifteen thousand, six hundred and twelve
5 one million, two hundred thousand
6 eighty-six thousand, three hundred and twenty-one
7 one/a hundred and fifteen thousand, two hundred
8 two hundred thousand, one hundred and nine
9 nine thousand, nine hundred and ninety-nine
10 five million, five hundred and fifty-five thousand, five hundred and fifty five

2
1 8,850 2 190 3 770 4 6,671 5 122 6 600 million / 600,000,000
7 1,600 8 3,000 and 8,000 9 155 million / 155,000,000
10 100,000 and 150,000

3a

```
┌─┐       ┌─┐─┬─┬─┐
│¹│       │²│ │ │ │
│C│       │G│A│V│E│
├─┤─┬─┐   └─┘ │ │
│³│ │ │     │ │
│A│T│E│     │ │
└─┘ └─┘     │ │
 │M│     ┌⁴┐ │ │
        │W│O│N│
 ┌⁵┐─┬─┬─┬─┬─┐
 │B│E│C│A│M│E│
 └─┘ └─┘ │ │ │
 │O│     │N│ ┌⁶┐
              │S│
 │U│   ┌⁷┐┌⁸┐─┬─┐
       │L││T│O│O│K│
 │G│   │E││ │ │ │
       ┌⁹┐─┬─┬─┐
 │H│   │F│O│U│N│D│
       └─┘ └─┘ └─┘
 │T│   │T│
```

3b
1 bought 2 went 3 saw 4 said 5 met 6 gave 7 found

4
1 got 2 didn't go 3 said 4 didn't have 5 went 6 looked 7 was
8 bought 9 did he buy 10 didn't buy 11 bought

5
3 Some people borrow money from friends.
4 Everyone gives a tip.
5 Most people save money every month.
6 No one invests money in shares.
7 Everyone buys things online.

6a

	Alex	Caterina
full name:	Alex Tew	Caterina Fake
nationality:	British	American
websites:	Million Dollar Homepage	Flickr and Hunch

6b
1 He sold pixels on his website for $1 each. 2 He earned $1,037,100.
3 People can put their photos on *Flickr* and other people can see them.
4 *Yahoo!* bought *Flickr*. 5 They paid $35 million. 6 She worked for *Yahoo!*

Unit 10

Lesson 10.1

1
1 get 2 move 3 learn 4 leave 5 get 6 graduate 7 fall 8 get/meet
9 retire 10 have 11 go 12 quit/start

2
1 She's going to have a baby. 2 He's going to get fit.
3 He's going to go to university. 4 He's going to retire.
5 She's going to start her own business. 6 They're going to get married.

3
1 'm going to move to a hot country 2 'm going to go to bed
3 's going to find a new job 4 're going to go to the beach
5 's going to be rich 6 's going to cook dinner 7 're going to move
8 'm going to dance

4
1 **A:** We're going to have a baby.
  B: Really? My best friend's going to have a baby, too.
2 **A:** My sons are going to go to university.
  B: Really? My daughter's going to go to university, too.
3 **A:** Davina's going to learn to drive.
  B: Really? I'm going to learn to drive, too.
4 **A:** Mr Ramos is going to start his own business.
  B: Really? You're going to start your own business, too.
5 **A:** I'm going to get fit.
  B: Really? My brother's going to get fit, too.
6 **A:** They're going to leave home next month.
  B: Really? We're going to leave home next month, too.

5a

A 2 B 3 C 1

5b

1 B 2 A and C 3 A and B 4 B and C 5 A

Lesson 10.2

1a

1b

1 I feel bored. 2 I feel excited. 3 I feel nervous. 4 I feel angry.
5 I feel tired. 6 I feel happy. 7 I feel upset. 8 I feel scared.

2a

1　He's going to do a lot of exercise. He isn't going to surf the
　　Internet every evening.
2　We're going to move house. We aren't going to watch a lot of TV.
3　She's going to get a new job. She isn't going to go out every night.
4　They're going to travel abroad. They aren't going to buy a new car.

2b

1　Are your parents going to buy a new car?
　　No, they aren't.
2　Is your husband going to surf the Internet every evening?
　　No, he isn't.
3　Are you and your husband going to move?
　　Yes, we are.
4　Is your sister going to go out every night?
　　No, she isn't,
5　Are your parents going to travel abroad?
　　Yes, they are.
6　Is your husband going to do a lot of exercise?
　　Yes, he is.

3

1 I'm not going to pay 2 Are you going to say 3 When are you going
to get married 4 We aren't going to be 5 We're going to be 6 You're
going to be 7 we're going to get 8 We aren't going to have 9 Where
are you going to have

4

1 tomorrow 2 Bye 3 weekend 4 Have a nice evening

5a

1 Are you going to have a party? 2 Where are you going to live?
3 Is she going to change jobs? 4 Who's going to tell him?

6a

[1] go to university [2] graduate [3] start a business
[4] earn a lot of money [5] retire early [6] relax [7] buy a boat

6b

1 are you going to do 2 sort of 3 are you going to do with
4 what are you going to do/your free time 5 are you going to do that

Lesson 10.3

1

1　**A:** Why are you upset?
　　B: Because I'm broke.
2　**A:** Why was Karen excited?
　　B: Because she booked a holiday to Italy.
3　**A:** Why do your sisters live at home?
　　B: Because they haven't got any money.
4　**A:** Why did you get married?
　　B: Because we were in love.
5　**A:** Why did Henri borrow a lot of money?
　　B: Because he wanted to buy a new car.

2

1　I joined the gym because I wanted to get fit.
2　I bought a new car because my old car was awful.
3　Why did/does your mother want to move?
4　Our cousins didn't go to university because they wanted to get a job.
5　I sold my CD player because I get all my music from the Internet now.
6　Why did Christine borrow €5?
7　Why were you late for class yesterday?
8　David quit his job because he was bored.

3

1　**A:** Why did she cycle up the hill?
　　B: Because she wanted to get fit.
2　**A:** Why did he start playing chess?
　　B: Because his grandfather was good at it.
3　**A:** Why did he jump out of the plane?
　　B: Because he had a parachute.
4　**A:** Why did he read the book?
　　B: Because it was interesting.

4a

1　**A:** Why did you buy her a clock?
　　B: Because she's always late.
2　**A:** Why did you join the gym?
　　B: Because I want to get fit.
3　**A:** Why did you buy that toy?
　　B: Because my sister's going to have a baby.
4　**A:** Why do you watch so much TV?
　　B: Because I like it.

5a

5b

1 jewellery 2 photo frame 3 tickets for a show 4 clock 5 chocolates

6

1 Oh 2 You're 3 These 4 Thank 5 Don't

Review and consolidation units 9–10

1

1 worked 2 liked 3 borrowed 4 lived 5 looked 6 cleaned
7 changed 8 danced

2

1 got 2 spent 3 said 4 helped 5 lent 6 sold 7 borrowed 8 washed

3

1 did, have/had 2 Did, go/didn't go/went 3 did, buy/bought
4 Did, take/didn't/took 5 did, meet/met 6 did, see/saw
7 came/did, come